Jo's Little Favorites III

~ Enduring Designs for Classic-Quilt Lovers ~

Jo Morton

Martingale
Create with Confidence

Jo's Little Favorites III: Enduring Designs for Classic-Quilt Lovers
© 2018 by Jo Morton

Martingale®
19021 120th Ave. NE, Ste. 102
Bothell, WA 98011-9511 USA
ShopMartingale.com

Printed in China
23 22 21 20 19 18   8 7 6 5 4 3 2 1

Library of Congress Cataloging-in-Publication Data is available upon request.

ISBN: 978-1-60468-904-4.

MISSION STATEMENT

We empower makers who use fabric and yarn to make life more enjoyable.

CREDITS

PUBLISHER AND
CHIEF VISIONARY OFFICER
Jennifer Erbe Keltner

CONTENT DIRECTOR
Karen Costello Soltys

MANAGING EDITOR
Tina Cook

ACQUISITIONS EDITOR
Karen M. Burns

TECHNICAL EDITOR
Ellen Pahl

COPY EDITOR
Jennifer Hornsby

DESIGN MANAGER
Adrienne Smitke

COVER DESIGNER
Regina Girard

INTERIOR DESIGNER
Angie Hoogensen

STUDIO PHOTOGRAPHER
Brent Kane

LOCATION PHOTOGRAPHER
Adam Albright

ILLUSTRATOR
Sandy Loi

APRIL 2018

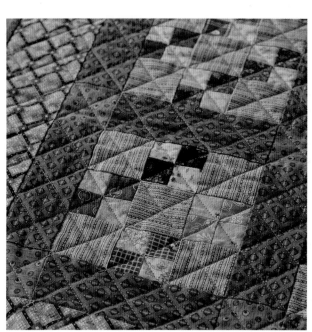

contents

introduction

Many people have asked me over the years why I prefer making small quilts. It's not as if I don't like bigger quilts. I do make them, and we always have a quilt on our bed and in the guest room. But as you'll see when you flip through the pages of this book (which was photographed in our home), I like to make quilts that I can use throughout my home.

Our small bungalow is filled with antique and reproduction furniture. Before buying any cupboard, dry sink, or table, I made sure I really loved it and knew where I could use it in our house. Years later, I still remember where and from whom I purchased each piece, and I wouldn't change a thing.

Not only have I enjoyed decorating our home with these beautiful and useful furniture pieces, but I also truly enjoy collecting handmade items. Whether old or new, from cloth, wood, pottery, tin, pewter, woven reed, or stitched, all of these items have a different feel than manufactured items do.

Walking into our home, visitors aren't overwhelmed by quilts. But if you'd take a moment to count the number of quilts in a single room, you might be surprised that there are well over a dozen: some in a folded stack, one underneath a box atop the jelly

cupboard, others in the bottom of the dry sink with pantry boxes, rolled into a candle box, custom framed on the wall, draped over the back of a wing chair, and more. Yet the quilts don't overtake the room. They are part of the setting, but not necessarily the focus.

I've always said I make the quilts for me and our home, and then I share them with you. So I hope you like what you see! Make them in your favorite colors for *your* home. And don't just stop at one or two. As you can see, no matter the size of your house, there's always room for another small quilt!

ANTIQUITY

Materials

Yardage is based on 42"-wide fabric. Fat quarters are 18" × 21". Fat eighths are 9" × 21".

⅓ yard *total* of assorted light prints for blocks
⅓ yard *total* of assorted dark prints for blocks
1 fat quarter of yellow print for inner border
1 fat quarter of teal print for outer border
1 fat eighth of navy print for single-fold binding
⅝ yard of fabric for backing
19" × 25" piece of batting

Cutting

From the assorted shirtings or light prints, cut:
20 squares, 3¼" × 3¼"

From the assorted dark prints, cut:
20 squares, 3¼" × 3¼"

From the *lengthwise* grain of the yellow print, cut:*
2 strips, 1" × 16½"
2 strips, 1" × 11½"

From the *lengthwise* grain of the teal print, cut:
2 strips, 2¼" × 17½"
2 strips, 2¼" × 15"

From the navy print, cut:
5 strips, 1⅛" × 21"

*I fussy cut the strips for my quilt. You may not need or want to, depending on your fabric.

Making the Blocks

Press all seam allowances as indicated by the arrows.

Quilting templates, whether vintage or reproductions, can provide inspiration for quilting designs and appliqué shapes.

Tin quilting shapes are peculiar to Pennsylvania and New England, so I'm always on the lookout for them when I travel to that part of the country. I love collecting and displaying them alongside my little quilts.

This quilt came into being when I was working on another project and I cut a few too many pieces. Well, you might say that I cut way too many! What to do? Make a small quilt with the extras, especially since I like these colors so much. My version fits nicely into the top of our antique dry sink for a little surprise when you walk by.

1. Draw a diagonal line from corner to corner on the wrong side of the light 3¼" squares. Align a marked light square with a dark print 3¼" square, right sides together. Sew a scant ¼" from each side of the drawn line. Cut on the line, and carefully press to make two half-square-triangle units. Make a total of 40 units.

Make 40 units.

Finished quilt: 15" × 21"
Finished block: 2" × 2"

~

*Pieced by Jo Morton and
quilted by Maggi Honeyman*

2. Pair two half-square-triangle units. Draw a diagonal line from corner to corner on the wrong side of one of the units as shown. Align the units with right sides together, with a light print facing a dark print, and butt the seams together. Sew a scant ¼" from each side of the drawn line. Cut on the line; use the "Clipping Trick" on page 90 at the seam intersection, and press seam allowances toward the darker fabric. Make a total of 40 Hourglass blocks that measure 2½" square.

Make 40 blocks,
2½" × 2½".

Assembling the Quilt Top

1. Arrange the Hourglass blocks in eight rows of five blocks each, referring to the assembly diagram. Rotate the blocks so that there is a light side against a dark side; double-check your layout before sewing. When satisfied with the

arrangement, sew the blocks into rows and press. Join the rows in pairs to make four two row units and press.

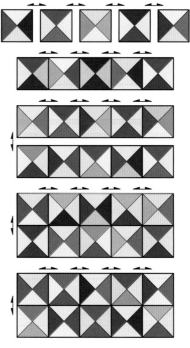

Quilt assembly

2. Join the two-row units into pairs and press, and then sew the two four-row units together; press. I find this assembly method easier to handle than adding rows one at a time. The quilt top should measure 10½" × 16½", including seam allowances.

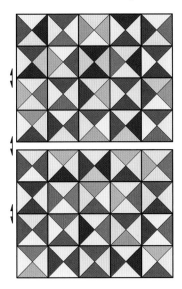

Adding the Borders

1. Pin and sew the yellow print 1" × 16½" strips to opposite sides of the quilt top and press. Pin and sew the yellow print 1" × 11½" strips to the top and bottom of the quilt top and press. The quilt top should measure 11½" × 17½", including seam allowances.

∾ pressing details ∾

I don't press seam allowances open very often, but it works for this quilt because of the way I wanted it to be quilted. The pressing of the Hourglass blocks creates a "ditch" on the diagonal, and that's where I planned to have the quilting. Pressing open works beautifully and distributes the bulk of the seam allowances.

∾

2. Pin and sew the teal print 2¼" × 17½" strips to opposite sides of the quilt top and press. Pin and sew the teal print 2¼" × 15" strips to the top and bottom of the quilt top and press. The quilt top should measure 15" × 21".

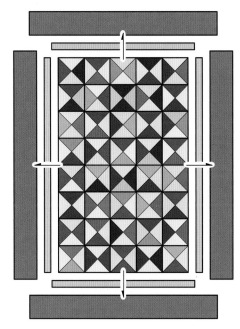

Adding borders

Finishing the Quilt

For more detailed information about any finishing steps, visit ShopMartingale.com/HowtoQuilt.

1. Layer the quilt top, batting, and backing. Baste the layers together.

2. Hand or machine quilt as desired. The quilt shown is quilted edge to edge following the diagonal of the Hourglass blocks, creating a crosshatched grid across the entire quilt.

3. Use the navy print 1⅛"-wide strips to make and attach single-fold binding (see "Single-Fold Binding" on page 94).

4. Make and attach a hanging sleeve, if desired.

5. Make, sign, and date a label and attach it to the back of your quilt.

BEDFORD REELS

Materials

Yardage is based on 42"-wide fabric. Fat quarters are 18" × 21".

1 yard *total* of assorted light prints for blocks
　　and border 2
1⅛ yards *total* of assorted medium to dark prints
　　for blocks and border 2
1 fat quarter of green print for setting triangles
⅞ yard of red print for border 1
1 yard of pink print for border 3
1⅛ yards of red floral for border 4
¼ yard of red stripe for single-fold binding
1⅛ yards of fabric for backing
40" × 40" piece of batting

Cutting

From the assorted light prints, cut:
16 squares, 5" × 5"
9 squares, 3½" × 3½", for reel appliqués
9 squares, 4" × 4", for jack appliqués
38 squares, 2¼" × 2¼"
2 squares, 1¾" × 1¾"

From the assorted medium to dark prints, cut:
9 squares, 5" × 5"
16 squares, 3½" × 3½", for reel appliqués
16 squares, 4" × 4", for jack appliqués
38 squares, 2¼" × 2¼"
2 squares, 1¾" × 1¾"

From the green print, cut:
3 squares, 7½" × 7½"; cut into quarters diagonally to
　　make 12 triangles
2 squares, 4¼" × 4¼"; cut in half diagonally to make
　　4 triangles

From the *lengthwise* grain of the red print, cut:
2 strips, 1¼" × 23⅛"
2 strips, 1¼" × 24⅝"

Continued on page 12

I love these petite appliquéd Reel blocks, and this quilt provides a beautiful setting for them. Think of stitching these blocks as your take-along project—you'll have them done sooner than you think.

　　The quilt was named for Bedford, Pennsylvania, where I've done quite a bit of antiquing over the years at folk-art shows. Blanket chests and painted boxes, like these in my living room, always appeal to me. They have a simple beauty and do double duty storing quilts that aren't on display.

　　Consider your own heirlooms, artwork, or collections as inspiration. Choose your palette and begin this beautiful journey.

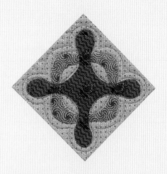

Finished quilt: 36⅛" × 36⅛"
Finished block: 4" × 4"

~

*Pieced and appliquéd by Jo Morton
and quilted by Lori Kukuk*

Continued from page 11

From the *lengthwise* grain of the pink print, cut:*
2 strips, 1¼" × 27⅛"
2 strips, 1¼" × 28⅝"

From the *lengthwise* grain of the red floral, cut:
2 strips, 4¼" × 28⅝"
2 strips, 4¼" × 36⅛"

From the red stripe, cut:
4 strips, 1⅛" × 42"

**I fussy cut these border strips, but you may not want
or need to, depending on your fabric.*

Appliquéing the Blocks

I appliquéd the blocks using my favorite method,
back-basting appliqué. If you use this technique, you
do not need to create templates or cut the appliqué
shapes beforehand. You'll find how-to information

for this technique beginning on page 90, and the
appliqué patterns are on page 15. You can, of course,
use your own preferred method of appliqué.

1. Using the pattern for the reel and a medium or
   dark 3½" square, appliqué the shape to a light
   print 5" background square. Using the pattern
   for the jack and a medium or dark 4" square,
   appliqué the shape to the background. I used
   two fabrics for some of the appliqués and just
   one fabric for others.

2. After the stitching is complete, trim the appliqué
   block to 4½" × 4½", including the seam allowances.
   Make 16 blocks with light backgrounds and 9
   blocks with medium or dark backgrounds.

Make 16 blocks;   Make 9 blocks;
trim to 4½" × 4½".   trim to 4½" × 4½".

Assembling the Quilt Top

Press all seam allowances as indicated by the arrows.

1. Referring to the assembly diagram below, arrange the blocks with light backgrounds on point in four rows of four blocks each. Fill in the nine openings with the blocks that have dark backgrounds. Add the green print 7½" setting triangles along all four edges. Sew into diagonal rows. Press the seam allowances toward the dark background blocks and toward the setting triangles.

2. Pin, matching seam intersections, and then sew the rows together. Use the "Clipping Trick" on page 90 at the seam intersections to press the seam allowances toward the dark background blocks and toward the setting triangles. Press the clipped intersections open. Sew a green print 4¼"

half-square triangle to each corner of the top, and press. Trim and square the quilt center to measure 23⅛" × 23⅛", including seam allowances.

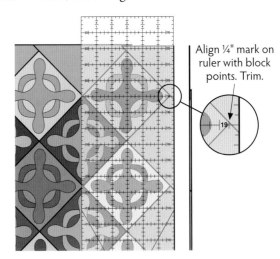

Align ¼" mark on ruler with block points. Trim.

Trim center to 23⅛" × 23⅛".

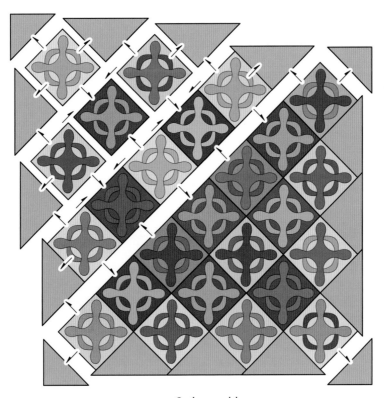

Quilt assembly

Adding the Borders

1. Pin and sew the red print 1¼" × 23⅛" strips to opposite sides of the quilt top. Press. Pin and sew the red print 1¼" × 24⅝" strips to the top and bottom of the quilt top and press. The quilt top should measure 24⅝" square, including seam allowances.

2. Pair a dark and a light 2¼" square. Draw a diagonal line from corner to corner on the wrong side of the light square. Align the squares with right sides together and sew a scant ¼" from each side of the drawn line. Cut on the drawn line and carefully press. Repeat with all of the 2¼" squares to make 76 half-square-triangle units. Trim each unit to measure 1¾" square.

Make 76 units.

3. Arrange the half-square-triangle units around the quilt center with the light triangles toward the center. There should be 19 units per side. Add the four 1¾" corner squares, with the dark and the light in opposite corners; the dark squares should be next to light triangles and the light squares should be next to dark triangles.

4. Sew each group of 19 half-square-triangle units together in a row to make four border strips (see "Fitting Finesse," above right). Carefully press the seam allowances open to distribute the bulk. The border strips should measure 24⅝" in length. Add the 1¾" squares to the ends of two of the strips and press.

Make 2 of each border.

5. Pin and sew the short borders to opposite sides of the quilt top, with light sides toward the center. Carefully press seam allowances toward the center of the quilt. Pin and sew the long borders to the top and bottom of the quilt top, with light sides

∾ fitting finesse ∾

The math isn't exact for the half-square-triangle border, as 19 × 1¼" = 24¼", including seam allowances. The quilt center should measure 24⅝", so take a few scant seam allowances as necessary when sewing each group of 19 half-square-triangle units together, and it should work just fine.

toward the center. Press, using the clipping trick at the corner seam intersections. Continue to press toward the border and press the clipped intersections open. The quilt top should measure 27⅛" square, including seam allowances.

6. Pin and sew the two pink print 1¼" × 27⅛" strips to opposite sides of the quilt and press. Pin and sew the two pink print 1¼" × 28⅝" strips to the top and bottom of the quilt and press. The top should now measure 28⅝" square, including seam allowances.

7. Pin and sew the two red floral 4¼" × 28⅝" strips to the sides of the quilt top and press. Pin and sew the red floral 4¼" × 36⅛" strips to the top and bottom of the quilt top and press. The quilt top should measure 36⅛" square.

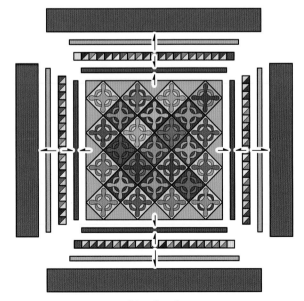

Adding borders

Finishing the Quilt

For more detailed information about any finishing steps, visit ShopMartingale.com/HowtoQuilt.

1. Layer the quilt top, batting, and backing. Baste the layers together.

2. Hand or machine quilt as desired. The quilt shown is machine quilted in the ditch around each reel, with a line of echo quilting about ¼" away. The green setting triangles are quilted in a chevron pattern. The inner red border, triangle border, and pink border are quilted in the ditch on both sides. There is a beautiful feather quilted in the red floral border. Thread colors were changed throughout the quilting to coordinate with the fabrics.

3. Use the red stripe 1⅛"-wide strips to make and attach single-fold binding (see "Single-Fold Binding" on page 94).

4. Make and attach a hanging sleeve, if desired.

5. Make, sign, and date a label and attach it to the back of your quilt.

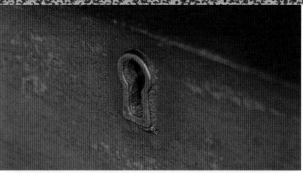

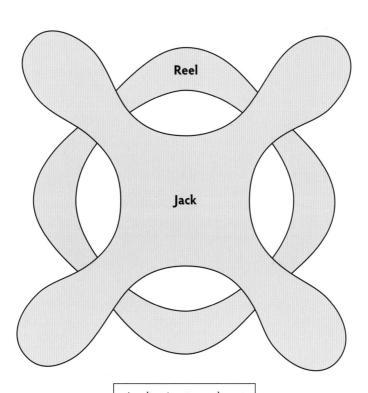

Reel

Jack

Appliqué patterns do not include seam allowances.

Materials

Yardage is based on 42"-wide fabric. Fat quarters are 18" × 21"; fat eighths are 9" × 21".

¼ yard *total* of assorted dark prints for blocks
¼ yard *total* of assorted light prints for blocks
1 fat quarter of gray stripe for blocks
1 fat quarter of brown print for sashing
1 fat eighth of cheddar print for sashing cornerstones
⅔ yard of tan print for border
1 fat eighth or scraps of brown stripe for border
    cornerstones
¼ yard of red print for single-fold binding
⅞ yard of fabric for backing
29" × 29" piece of batting

Cutting

From the assorted dark prints, cut:
36 *matching pairs* of squares, 1¼" × 1¼" (72 total)

From the assorted light prints, cut:
36 *matching pairs* of squares, 1¼" × 1¼" (72 total)

From the gray stripe, cut:
5 strips, 2" × 21"; crosscut into 45 squares, 2" × 2"

From the brown print, cut:
3 strips, 5" × 21"; crosscut into 24 strips, 2" × 5"

From the cheddar print, cut:
2 strips, 2" × 21"; crosscut into 16 squares, 2" × 2"

From the *lengthwise* grain of the tan print, cut:
4 strips, 3" × 20"

From the brown stripe, cut:
4 squares, 3" × 3"

From the red print, cut:
3 strips, 1⅛" × 42"

Here's another delightful design to use up small pieces. Most of the four patches were made with two fabrics, a light and a dark, but sometimes I had odds and ends, so there are three-fabric blocks also. I wanted scrappy! The gray stripe in the blocks adds vintage charm (no, I don't always worry about which direction the stripes run), and this quilt looks wonderful as a table topper with a grouping of antiques or other treasures. The brown sashing print gives it warmth and inspired the name, Brown Sugar. It reminds me of baking for the holidays. The simple crosshatch quilting is a traditional design and one used frequently on useful everyday quilts like this one.

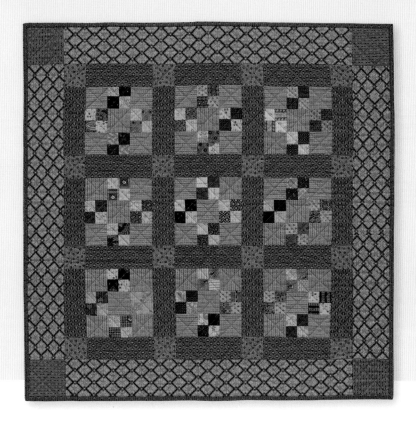

Finished quilt: 25" × 25"
Finished four-patch unit: 1½" × 1½"
Finished block: 4½" × 4½"

~

*Pieced by Jo Morton and
quilted by Maggi Honeyman*

Making the Blocks

Press all seam allowances as shown by the arrows in
the illustrations.

1. Arrange two matching light 1¼" squares and two
   matching dark 1¼" squares to form a four-patch
   unit. Sew the squares together in pairs and press.
   Sew the pairs together and press to make a
   four-patch unit that measures 2" square, including
   seam allowances. Make 36.

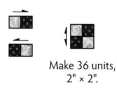

Make 36 units,
2" × 2".

2. Arrange four of the four-patch units and five
   gray stripe 2" squares to form a Nine Patch
   block. Sew into rows and press. Join the rows,
   matching seam intersections. Use the "Clipping

Trick" on page 90 at the seam intersections and
press. Make nine blocks that measure 5" square,
including seam allowances.

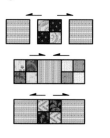

Make 9 blocks,
5" × 5".

~ **clipping trick** ~

*Use my "Clipping Trick" on page 90 to press
seam intersections into little four patches. This
allows you to press toward the unpieced squares
for a smooth quilt top.*

~

Assembling the Quilt Top

1. Referring to the assembly diagram, arrange the blocks in three rows of three blocks each, alternating them with four brown print 2" × 5" sashing strips. Add sashing strips and cheddar 2" squares between the block rows. Sew the blocks and sashing into rows and press. Pin the rows, matching seam intersections, and sew. Use the clipping trick again at the seam intersections and press. The quilt center should measure 20" square, including seam allowances.

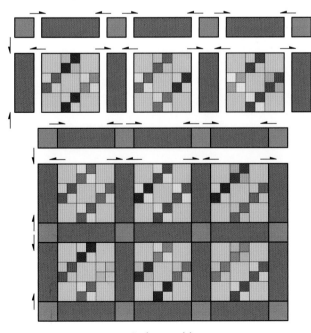

Quilt assembly

2. Pin and sew two tan print 3" × 20" strips to the sides of the quilt and press. Sew the brown stripe 3" squares to each end of the remaining tan strips and press. Pin and sew these borders to the top and bottom of the quilt. Use the clipping trick at the seam intersections and press. The quilt top should measure 25" square.

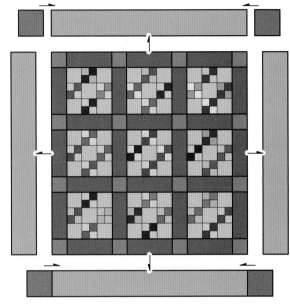

Adding border

Finishing the Quilt

For more detailed information about any finishing steps, visit ShopMartingale.com/HowtoQuilt.

1. Layer the quilt top, batting, and backing. Baste the layers together.

2. Hand or machine quilt as desired. This quilt is quilted by machine in a crosshatch grid from edge to edge, using the four patches as a basis for the grid. It's the perfect old-fashioned quilting design for an old-fashioned quilt.

3. Use the red print 1⅛"-wide strips to make and attach single-fold binding (see "Single-Fold Binding" on page 94).

4. Make and attach a hanging sleeve, if desired.

5. Make, sign, and date a label and attach it to the back of your quilt.

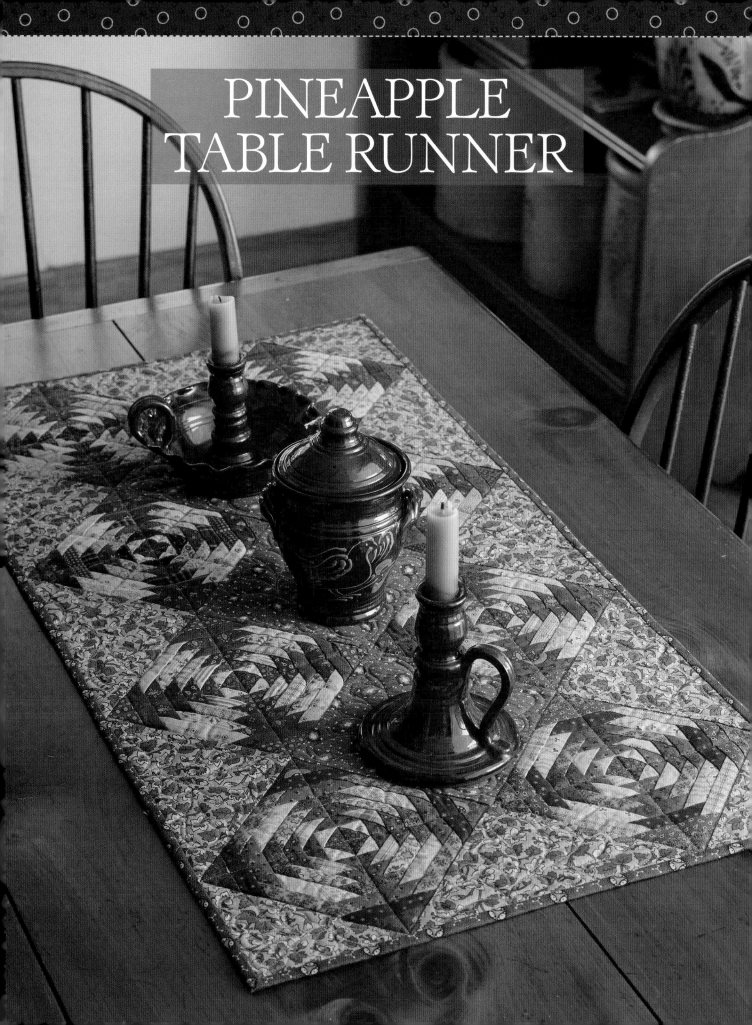

PINEAPPLE TABLE RUNNER

Materials

Yardage is based on 42"-wide fabric. Fat eighths are 9" × 21".

⅝ yard *total* of assorted red prints for blocks
¾ yard *total* of assorted cream prints for blocks
⅝ yard *total* of assorted brown prints for blocks
⅜ yard of tan floral for setting triangles
1 fat eighth of brown print for setting squares
¼ yard of red print for single-fold binding
⅝ yard of fabric for backing
22" × 39" piece of batting

Cutting

The number of strips needed for foundation piecing the blocks may vary. Keep your fabrics handy in case you need to cut more.

From the *lengthwise* grain of the assorted red prints, cut:
20 strips, 1" × 18"
4 strips, 2" × 18"
8 squares, 1½" × 1½"

From the *lengthwise* grain of the assorted cream prints, cut:
40 strips, 1" × 18"

From the *lengthwise* grain of the assorted brown prints, cut:
20 strips, 1" × 18"
4 strips, 2" × 18"

From the tan floral, cut:
2 squares, 10¼" × 10¼"; cut into quarters diagonally to make 8 triangles
2 squares, 5⅝" × 5⅝"; cut in half diagonally to make 4 triangles

From the brown print fat eighth, cut:
3 squares, 6½" × 6½"

From the red print yardage, cut:
3 strips, 1⅛" × 42"

The reds, browns, and tans in this table runner make it a perfect setting for redware and other vintage pottery. Plan for accessories that won't cover up all of your stunning patchwork. Setting squares on this runner are the ideal platform for two candleholders and a small lidded jar. I love the warm glow this combination of things adds to our bungalow dining room.

Worried about how you'll keep your seams straight with such small pieces? Fret no more! The blocks are paper pieced for ease of construction. If you've never tried your hand at paper piecing, this eight-block project is a great place to start.

Finished table runner: 17½" × 34½"
Finished block: 6" × 6"

~

*Pieced by Jo Morton and
quilted by Maggi Honeyman*

Foundation Piecing the Blocks

With paper foundation piecing, you sew the fabric pieces to paper on the reverse side of the block pattern. Sew on the lines on the printed side of the paper with the fabric on the unprinted side. Pieces are sewn in numerical order, so there is no guessing about what to sew next. Have a lamp or window close by so that you can hold up the paper foundation and fabric pieces to the light. This will allow you to check that you have the appropriate space adequately covered with fabric.

1. Make eight copies of the foundation pattern on page 25. You can use regular copy paper or purchase paper made especially for foundation piecing.

2. Set your sewing machine's stitch length to 1.5, or about 18 stitches per inch; this shorter stitch makes it easier to remove the papers after the block has been pieced and pressed.

3. Place a red 1½" center square right side up on the blank side of the paper, centering it over the center square, space 1. Do this by holding it up to the light, and then pin in place on the printed side.

Wrong side of pattern

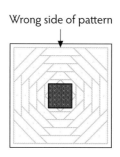

Right side of pattern

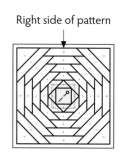

4. For space 2, choose a cream 1" × 18" strip and cut four pieces at least ½" longer than the space that you will be covering, about 1¾". It's easier to cut longer than needed, especially if you are new to paper piecing. Align the piece along the edge of the center square, with right sides together. Turn the paper over and sew exactly on the line. Sew a stitch or two past both ends of the line, or backstitch on both ends. Sew a second cream print strip on the opposite side of the square.

5. Turn the foundation over, fold the paper back, trim the seam allowances to ¼" and press.

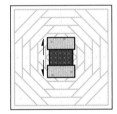

6. Repeat steps 4 and 5 to add the cream pieces to the remaining two sides, covering all of the space 2 areas.

7. For the next round, the space 3 areas, choose a red or brown print and repeat steps 4 and 5, cutting the strips so that they are at least ½" longer than the space to be covered. Note that I made half the blocks beginning with red, and half beginning with brown.

8. Continue in the same manner, using the 1"-wide strips to piece the block. Spaces 2, 4, 6, 8, and 10 should be cream. Spaces 3, 5, 7, 9, 11, and 12 are alternately red or brown. For the space 12 corner areas, use the 2"-wide strips.

∾ paper piecing tips ∾

- *I like using my Add-A-Quarter ruler to trim excess fabric when paper piecing. Fold the paper out of the way and trim, leaving a ¼" seam allowance.*

- *Use the same print strip for each round of the block; the fabric is used four times per round.*

- *Consider preselecting the fabrics you want in each block, and layer them in the order you want to use them.*

∾

9. Trim and square the block to measure 6½" × 6½", keeping the paper in place for now. Make a total of eight blocks: four that begin with a brown strip, and four that begin with a red strip.

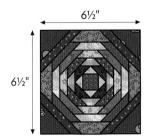

Make 4 of each block.

Assembling the Runner Top

1. Arrange the blocks on point in two vertical rows of four blocks each. Fill in with the brown 6½" squares and the tan floral 10¼" triangles. Sew into diagonal rows. Press. Pin, matching seam intersections, and sew the rows together. Use the "Clipping Trick" on page 90 at the seam intersections to press seam allowances toward the setting squares and triangles. Sew the four tan floral 5⅝" triangles to the corners and press.

2. Carefully remove the paper from the wrong side of the blocks and press the runner.

3. Trim the excess fabric from the sides, leaving a ¼" seam allowance beyond the block points. The runner top should measure 17½" × 34½".

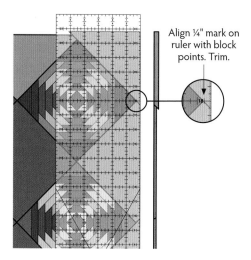

Align ¼" mark on ruler with block points. Trim.

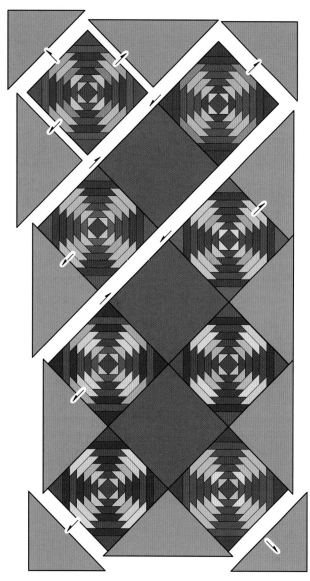

Runner assembly

Finishing the Table Runner

For more detailed information about any finishing steps, visit ShopMartingale.com/HowtoQuilt.

1. Layer the quilt top, batting, and backing. Baste the layers together.

2. Hand or machine quilt as desired. The quilt shown features a beautiful square feathered wreath in the three brown print squares. Half and quarter designs are used in the setting triangles. The Pineapple blocks are quilted with an X from corner to corner over the block and two rows of stitching in the ditch.

3. Use the red print 1⅛"-wide strips to make and attach single-fold binding (see "Single-Fold Binding" on page 94).

4. Make and attach a hanging sleeve, if desired.

5. Make, sign, and date a label and attach it to the back of your quilt.

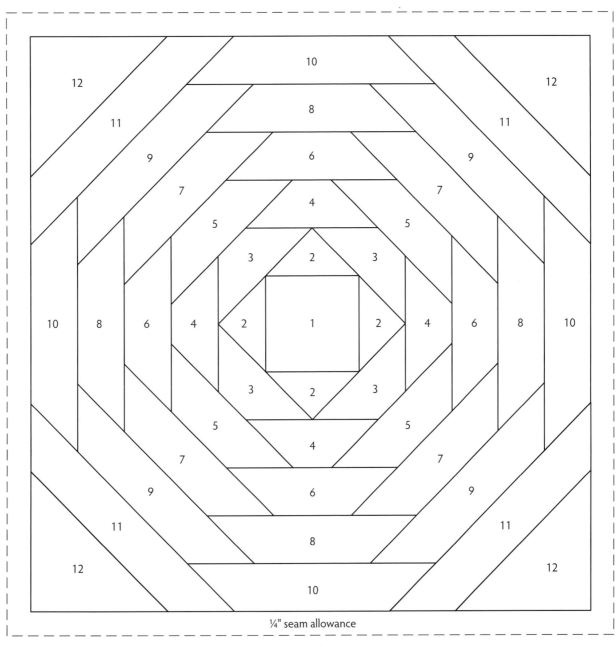

¼" seam allowance

Pineapple foundation pattern
Make 8 copies.

STAR SHINE

I love star quilts, and from the chatter on social media, it seems many other quilters do too. We quilters are starstruck! This quilt has just what the doctor ordered: lovely, easy-to-piece Star blocks set on point with all the bells and whistles of sashing, cornerstones, and a pieced border.

Hang this quilt on the wall for best display, or use it on a larger table if wall space is limited. I live in a small house—1,100 square feet—so nearly all of my accessories double as storage. But pantry boxes like these in the photo are more artful and pleasing to me than plastic bins. My advice? Make sure to enjoy your storage solutions whenever and wherever possible.

Materials

Yardage is based on 42"-wide fabric.

⅜ yard *total* of assorted peach, cream, red, blue, gold, and brown prints for blocks
⅜ yard of muslin for blocks
⅞ yard of beige print for sashing and outer border
⅛ yard of indigo print for sashing cornerstones
½ yard of brown stripe for setting triangles, border cornerstones, and single-fold binding
⅛ yard of cream print for pieced border
⅛ yard *each* of 3 assorted red prints for pieced border
1 yard of fabric for backing
34" × 34" piece of batting

Cutting

From the assorted prints for blocks, cut:
13 *matching sets* of 4 squares, 1⅞" × 1⅞" (52 total)
13 squares, 2½" × 2½"

From the muslin, cut:
2 strips, 3¼" × 42"; crosscut into 13 squares, 3¼" × 3¼"
2 strips, 1½" × 42"; crosscut into 52 squares, 1½" × 1½"

From the *lengthwise* grain of the beige print, cut:*
4 strips, 3½" × 23½"
36 strips, 1½" × 4½"

From the indigo print, cut:
1 strip, 1½" × 42"; crosscut into 24 squares, 1½" × 1½"

From the brown stripe, cut:
2 squares, 8¼" × 8¼"; cut into quarters diagonally to make 8 triangles
2 squares, 5" × 5"; cut in half diagonally to make 4 triangles**
4 squares, 1⅜" × 1⅜"
4 squares, 3½" × 3½"
4 strips, 1⅛" × 42"

Cut the 3½"-wide strips first. Then cut the rectangles.

**If you are using a stripe and want all the stripes to run in the same direction, cut the second square with the diagonal going in the opposite direction of the first.*

Continued on page 28

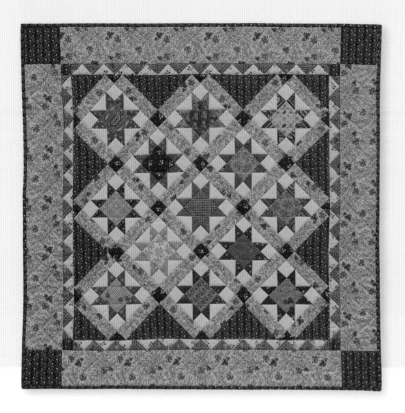

Finished quilt: 29½" × 29½"
Finished block: 4" × 4"

~

*Pieced by Jo Morton and
quilted by Maggi Honeyman*

Continued from page 27

From the cream print, cut:

1 strip, 3" × 42"; crosscut into 12 squares, 3" × 3"

From *each of 3* assorted red prints, cut:

16 squares, 1¾" × 1¾" (48 total)

Making the Blocks

The instructions are written to make one block at a time. Press all seam allowances as shown by the arrows in the illustrations.

1. Select the following for one block:

   - 1 set of 4 matching print 1⅞" squares for star points
   - 1 muslin 3¼" square and 4 muslin 1½" squares for background
   - 1 print 2½" square for the star center

2. Draw a diagonal line from corner to corner on the wrong side of the four assorted print 1⅞" squares. Align two marked squares on opposite corners of a muslin 3¼" square, right sides together. The squares will overlap in the center. Sew a scant ¼" from each side of the drawn lines. Cut on the drawn lines. Press carefully; do not stretch the fabrics.

Make 2 units.

3. Align a marked square on the corner of a muslin triangle, noting the direction of the diagonal line. Sew a scant ¼" from each side of the line. Cut on the line and press. Repeat to make four matching flying-geese units that measure 1½" × 2½", including seam allowances.

Make 4 units,
1½" × 2½".

4. Arrange the flying-geese units, four muslin 1½" squares, and a print 2½" square in three rows as shown. Sew into rows and press. Pin the rows, matching seam intersections, and sew. Press to complete the block; it should measure 4½" square, including seam allowances. Use the "Clipping Trick" on page 90 at the seam intersections. Press the background corners toward the corner, press the center section toward the center, and press the seam intersections open. Make 13 blocks.

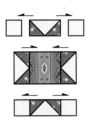

Make 13 blocks,
4½" × 4½".

Assembling the Quilt Top

1. Arrange nine Star blocks on point in rows of three across and three down. Place the remaining four Star blocks between the blocks, allowing room for the sashing strips and cornerstones.

❧ starring stripes ❧

If you're using a stripe for the side triangles, you can position the stripes to run vertically in the quilt, which adds nice subtle interest. Note that the setting triangles are cut slightly oversized.

2. Arrange the sashing strips to frame all the blocks, and add the cornerstones. Fill in with the brown side triangles. The cornerstones will be trimmed when the quilt center is squared up.

3. Sew the blocks and sashing strips in diagonal rows and press. Sew sashing strips and cornerstones to make diagonal rows and press.

4. Pin a sashing row to a block row, matching seam intersections, and sew. Use the clipping trick at the seam intersections and continue to press seam allowances toward the sashing strips. Press the clipped intersections open.

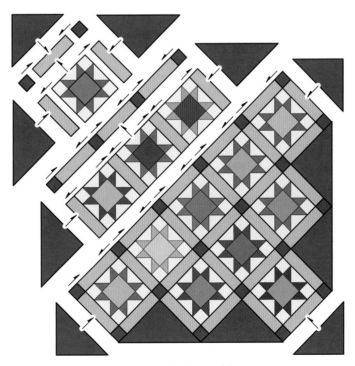

Quilt assembly

5. After the rows are joined, add the corner triangles and press the seam allowances toward the sashing strips.

6. Trim the edges of the quilt top, leaving a ¼" seam allowance; the outer cornerstones will appear to be halved when sewn. The top should measure 21¾" square, including seam allowances.

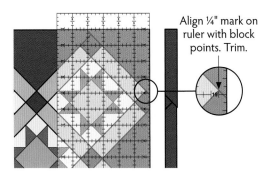

Align ¼" mark on ruler with block points. Trim.

Trim to 21¾" × 21¾".

Adding Flying-Geese Border

1. Draw a diagonal line from corner to corner on the wrong side of four matching red print 1¾" squares. Align two marked squares on opposite corners of a cream print 3" square, right sides together; the squares will overlap in the center. Sew a scant ¼" from each side of the drawn lines. Cut on the drawn lines. Press carefully; don't stretch fabrics.

Make 2 units.

2. Align a marked red square on the corner of one of the cream triangles, noting the direction of the diagonal line. Sew a scant ¼" from each side of the drawn line. Cut on the line and press. Repeat with the second unit to make four matching flying-geese units that measure 1⅜" × 2¼", including seam allowances. Make a total of 48 units.

Make 48 units, 1⅜" × 2¼".

3. Arrange 12 flying-geese units along each side of the quilt center, with the light edge toward the center. Carefully sew the units together with a scant ¼" seam allowance and press. Each strip needs to measure 21¾"; the exact length of the border strip based on the math is 21½", but with this many seams, it can be slightly stretched to fit. Pin and sew two of these pieced border strips to opposite sides of the quilt top, and carefully press.

4. Sew the brown stripe 1⅜" squares to the ends of the remaining two strips and press. Pin these strips to the top and bottom of the quilt and sew. Use the clipping trick at the corner seam intersections. Press the flying-geese seam allowances toward the quilt center and the squares seam allowances away from the center. Press the clipped intersection open. The quilt top should measure 23½" square, including seam allowances.

Adding pieced border

Adding the Outer Border

1. Pin and sew beige print 3½" × 23½" border strips to opposite sides of the quilt top and press.

2. Sew the brown stripe 3½" squares to the ends of the two remaining border strips and press. Pin and sew these borders to the top and bottom of the quilt, matching seam intersections, and press. The quilt top should measure 29½" square.

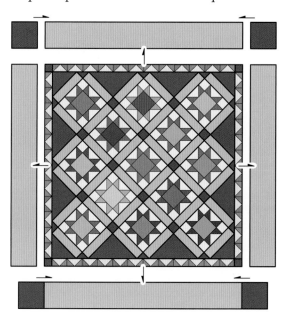

Adding outer border

Finishing the Quilt

For more detailed information about any finishing steps, visit ShopMartingale.com/HowtoQuilt.

1. Layer the quilt top, batting, and backing. Baste the layers together.

2. Hand or machine quilt as desired. The Star blocks in the quilt shown are quilted in the ditch, with a square in the center of each star. Sashing strips are quilted in the ditch and through the center. Cornerstones are quilted in the ditch only. A triangular feathered spray is quilted in the setting triangles. The borders are quilted in a crosshatch grid following the angle of the pink triangles in the pieced border.

3. Use the brown stripe 1⅛"-wide strips to make and attach single-fold binding (see "Single-Fold Binding" on page 94).

4. Make and attach a hanging sleeve, if desired.

5. Make, sign, and date a label and attach it to the back of your quilt.

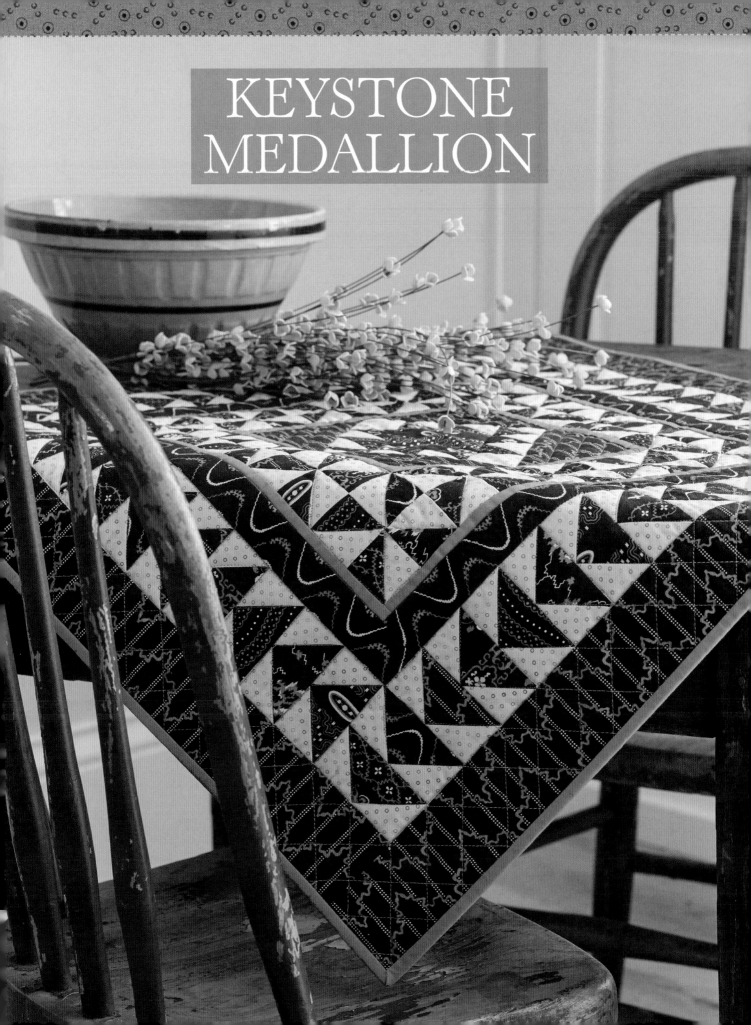

KEYSTONE MEDALLION

Materials

Yardage is based on 42"-wide fabric. Fat quarters are 18" × 21".

⅝ yard *total* of assorted indigo prints for center block, Pinwheel blocks, and flying-geese border
½ yard of cream print for block backgrounds
⅞ yard of indigo print A for setting triangles and outer border
1 fat quarter of cheddar solid for narrow borders
1 fat quarter of indigo print B for inner border
1 fat quarter of cheddar print for single-fold binding
⅞ yard of fabric for backing
29" × 29" piece of batting

Cutting

From the assorted indigo prints, cut:
1 square, 3" × 3"
5 squares, 2¼" × 2¼"
8 squares, 4½" × 4½"
14 squares, 3¾" × 3¾"

From the cream print, cut:
1 strip, 2¼" × 42"; crosscut into:
    5 squares, 2¼" × 2¼"
    2 squares, 1¾" × 1¾"
    11 squares, 2⅛" × 2⅛"
1 strip, 4½" × 42"; crosscut into 8 squares, 4½" × 4½"
3 strips, 2⅛" × 42"; crosscut into 45 squares,
    2⅛" × 2⅛"

From the *lengthwise* grain of indigo print A, cut:
2 strips, 2½" × 20½"
2 strips, 2½" × 24½"
2 squares, 4¾" × 4¾"; cut in half diagonally to make
    4 triangles

From the *lengthwise* grain of the cheddar solid, cut:
2 strips, 1" × 7½"
2 strips, 1" × 8½"
2 strips, 1" × 13"
2 strips, 1" × 14"

Quilters may think that larger-scale prints don't work in small quilts, but these prints can be wonderful in small pieces. Larger prints add movement. These indigo and cheddar prints make a stunning medallion-style quilt.

When decorating with small quilts, take a cue from the quilt's color story to choose your accessories. In this vignette using an antique children's table and chairs, two things catch my eye: The yellowware bowl has a subdued tone that lightens the overall setting without calling too much attention. And up close, the chipped paint on the chairs reveals a cheddary orange and a hint of blue. To my eye, it's these little pops of color that set the scene perfectly. When in season, a little pot of marigolds in this setting would be just right too.

Continued on page 34

Finished quilt: 24½" × 24½"
Finished Pinwheel block:
2½" × 2½"

~

Pieced by Jo Morton and
quilted by Maggi Honeyman

Continued from page 33

From the *lengthwise* grain of indigo print B, cut:
2 strips, 1½" × 13½"
2 strips, 1½" × 15½"

From the cheddar print, cut:
6 strips, 1⅛" × 21"

∾ reminder ∾

A "scant" ¼" seam means just a thread or two
shy of a full ¼" seam.

~

Making the Medallion Center

Press all seam allowances as shown by the arrows
in the illustrations.

1. Draw a diagonal line from corner to corner on the
   wrong side of the five cream print 2¼" squares.
   Align each marked cream square on an indigo 2¼"
   square, right sides together. Sew a scant ¼" from
   each side of the drawn line. Cut on the drawn line
   and carefully press to make 10 half-square-triangle
   units. Trim the units to measure 1¾" square.

Make 10 units.

2. Arrange the half-square-triangle units and two
   cream 1¾" squares around the indigo 3" center
   square as shown on page 35. Sew the half-square-
   triangle units into rows and press. Pin and sew the

short rows to opposite sides of the center dark square and press. Pin and sew the top and bottom rows to the center unit, matching seam intersections, and press. Use the "Clipping Trick" on page 90 at the seam intersections, and press the seam allowances toward the center square and toward the corners. Press the seam intersections open. The block should measure 5½" square, including seam allowances.

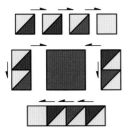

Make 1 block,
5½" × 5½".

3. Sew the indigo print A triangles to opposite sides of the center block and press the seam allowances toward the corners. Repeat with the remaining two corners. Trim the unit to measure 7½" square.

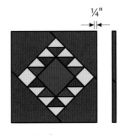

Make 1 unit,
7½" × 7½".

4. Pin and sew the two cheddar 1" × 7½" strips to opposite sides of the center unit and press. Pin and sew the two cheddar 1" × 8½" strips to the remaining sides of the unit and press. Evenly trim the unit to measure 8" square.

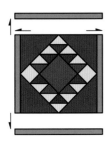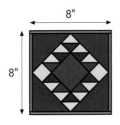

Make 1 unit.

∾ border trick ∾

I find it much easier and more accurate to add a wider border and trim it down, rather than try to evenly sew a narrow border to a quilt top.

∾

Making the Pinwheel Border

1. Draw a diagonal line from corner to corner in each direction to make an X on the wrong side of the eight cream 4½" squares. Layer each marked square with an indigo 4½" square, right sides together. Sew a scant ¼" from both sides of the drawn lines. Cut the units in half horizontally and vertically; then cut them on the diagonal lines and press to make total of 64 half-square-triangle units. Trim the units to measure 1¾" square.

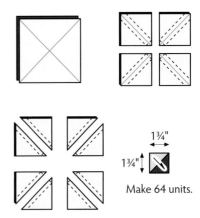

1¾"

1¾"

Make 64 units.

2. Arrange four half-square-triangle units to form a Pinwheel. Sew the units together in pairs and press. Pin and sew the pairs together, matching seam intersections. Use the clipping trick at the seam intersection to press seam allowances in a circular manner; press the clipped intersection open. The block should measure 3" square, including seam allowances. Make 16 Pinwheel blocks.

Make 16 blocks,
3" × 3".

3. Arrange the Pinwheel blocks around the quilt center. Sew into rows of three blocks for the sides and five blocks for the top and bottom. Press.

4. Pin and sew the side rows to the quilt center and press. Pin and sew the top and bottom rows to the quilt center, matching seam intersections, and press. Use the clipping trick at the four corners where the Pinwheels meet the center section and press the center three Pinwheel blocks toward the center. Press the outer Pinwheel block seam allowances open. Press the clipped intersection open. The quilt should measure 13" square, including seam allowances.

Adding Two Unpieced Borders

1. Pin and sew the cheddar 1" × 13" strips to opposite sides of the quilt center and press. Pin and sew the cheddar 1" × 14" strips to the top and bottom of the quilt center and press. Evenly trim and square the top to measure 13½" square, including seam allowances.

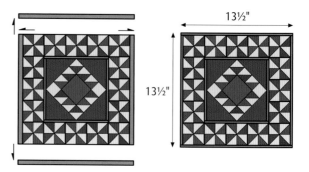

2. Pin and sew the 1½" × 13½" indigo print B strips to opposite sides of the quilt and press seam allowances toward the indigo print border. Pin and sew the indigo 1½" × 15½" strips to the top and bottom of the quilt and press. The quilt top should measure 15½" square, including seam allowances.

Making the Flying-Geese Border

1. Draw a diagonal line from corner to corner on the wrong side of four cream 2⅛" squares. Align two marked squares on opposite corners of an indigo 3¾" square, right sides together. The squares will overlap in the center. Sew a scant ¼" from each side of the drawn lines. Cut on the drawn lines and press.

Make 2 units.

2. Align a marked cream 2⅛" square on the corner of each indigo triangle, right sides together, noting the direction of the diagonal line. Sew a scant ¼" from each side of the drawn line. Cut on the line and press. Repeat with the second unit to make four identical flying-geese units. Trim the units to measure 1¾" × 3". Make a total of 56 flying-geese units.

Make 56 units,
1¾" × 3".

3. Sew 12 flying-geese units together as shown to make a side border and press. Make two side borders that measure 3" × 15½", including seam allowances.

Make 2 side borders,
3" × 15½".

4. Sew 16 flying-geese units together as shown and press. Make two top/bottom borders that measure 3" × 20½", including seam allowances.

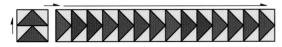

Make 2 top/bottom borders,
3" × 20½".

Adding the Outer Borders

1. Pin and sew the shorter flying-geese borders to opposite sides of the quilt, noting the direction of the flying geese in the quilt assembly diagram above right. Press.

2. Pin the longer flying-geese borders to the top and bottom of the quilt, double-check the direction of the flying geese, and sew. Press. The quilt top should measure 20½" square, including seam allowances.

3. Pin and sew the 2½" × 20½" indigo print A strips to opposite sides of the quilt and press. Pin and sew the 2½" × 24½" indigo A strips to the top and bottom of the quilt and press. The quilt top should measure 24½" square.

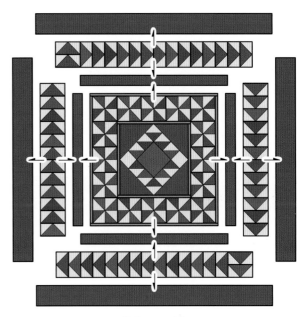

Quilt assembly

Finishing the Quilt

For more detailed information about any finishing steps, visit ShopMartingale.com/HowtoQuilt.

1. Layer the quilt top, batting, and backing. Baste the layers together.

2. Hand or machine quilt as desired. This quilt is stitched in the ditch of the center block with echoing parallel lines in the setting triangles. Crosshatching is stitched throughout the remainder of the quilt; the distance between lines was determined by the diagonals of the flying-geese units.

3. Use the cheddar print 1⅛"-wide strips to make and attach single-fold binding (see "Single-Fold Binding" on page 94).

4. Make and attach a hanging sleeve, if desired.

5. Make, sign, and date a label and attach it to the back of your quilt.

WINTER HARBOR

Materials

Yardage is based on 42"-wide fabric. Fat quarters are 18" × 21"; fat eighths are 9" × 21".

½ yard *total* of assorted brown prints for blocks
⅜ yard *total* of assorted cream prints for blocks
⅜ yard *total* of assorted red prints for blocks
1 fat quarter of cheddar print for sashing
1 fat eighth of brown print for cornerstones
1 yard of brown print for setting triangles and border
¼ yard of red print for single-fold binding
1 yard of fabric for backing
32" × 32" piece of batting

Cutting

From the assorted brown prints, cut:
13 *matching sets* of:
    2 squares, 2½" × 2½" (26 total)
    1 square, 1¾" × 1¾" (13 total)
    4 squares, 1⅜" × 1⅜" (52 total)

From the assorted cream prints, cut:
13 *matching sets* of:
    8 squares, 1½" × 1½" (104 total)
    4 squares, 1½" × 1½"; cut in half diagonally
      to make 8 triangles (104 total)

From the assorted red prints, cut:
13 squares, 4" × 4"; cut into quarters diagonally
    to make 52 triangles

From the *lengthwise* grain of the cheddar print, cut:
36 strips, 1½" × 4⅞"

From the brown print fat eighth, cut:
24 squares, 1½" × 1½"

From the *lengthwise* grain of the brown print yardage, cut:*
2 strips, 2¾" × 23¼"
2 strips, 2¾" × 27¾"
2 squares, 8⅝" × 8⅝"; cut into quarters diagonally to
    make 8 triangles
2 squares, 5¼" × 5¼"; cut in half diagonally to make
    4 triangles

From the red print, cut:
3 strips, 1⅛" × 42"

*For the most efficient use of your fabric, cut the pieces in the order listed.

I was teaching a class using the Wild Goose Chase block in a 9¾" size when a student wanted to make a much smaller version. Once I calculated the measurements, I made a test block, and that led to another block and another and another! This quilt is the result. I hand quilted it to add to the vintage appeal.

If you can't find the perfect table to display in your home, make one from found objects like these timeworn suitcases. Perhaps the top of the "table" isn't quite polished enough for your taste. Drape a quilt over the top to finish the look in a lovely way.

Finished quilt: 27¾" × 27¾"
Finished block: 4⅜" × 4⅜"

~

Pieced and quilted by
Jo Morton

Making the Blocks

The instructions are written to make one block at a time. Press all seam allowances as indicated by the arrows in the illustrations.

1. Select the following pieces for one block:
   - A matching set of 2 brown print 2½" squares, 1 brown print 1¾" square, and 4 brown print 1⅜" squares
   - A matching set of 8 cream print 1½" squares and 8 cream print 1½" triangles
   - 4 matching red print 4" triangles

2. Draw a diagonal line from corner to corner on the wrong side of the eight cream 1½" squares. Align two marked squares on opposite corners of a brown print 2½" square, right sides together. The squares will overlap in the center. Sew a scant ¼" from each side of the drawn lines. Cut on the drawn lines and press.

Make 2 units.

3. Align a marked cream square on the corner of one of the brown triangles, right sides together, noting the direction of the diagonal line. Sew a scant ¼" from each side of the drawn line. Cut on the marked line and press. Repeat to make eight flying-geese units that measure 1⅛" × 1¾".

Make 8 units,
1⅛" × 1¾".

4. Sew a cream print triangle to one side of a brown print 1⅜" square and press. Sew a second cream triangle to the adjacent side of the brown square and press. Make four of these corner units.

Make 4 units.

5. Sew two flying-geese units to a corner unit as shown. Press the seam allowances away from the corner unit. Make four units.

Make 4 units.

6. Arrange the units from step 5 with the red print triangles and the brown print 1¾" square as shown. Sew the pieces into rows and press. Pin and sew the rows together, matching seam intersections. Use the "Clipping Trick" on page 90 at the seam intersections and press the seam allowances toward the side triangles and center square. Press the clipped intersections open.

7. Trim and square the Wild Goose Chase block to measure 4⅞" square, including seam allowances. The side triangles were cut slightly oversized. Make a total of 13 blocks.

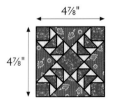

Make 13 blocks.

Assembling the Quilt Top

1. Referring to the quilt assembly diagram on page 42, arrange nine blocks on point in three rows of three blocks each. Then place the four remaining blocks between them, allowing space for the sashing strips and cornerstones. Add the cheddar print 1½" × 4⅞" sashing strips and the brown print 1½" squares. Fill in with brown print side triangles and corner triangles. Sew the blocks, sashing strips, and side triangles into diagonal rows and press. Sew the sashing strips and cornerstones to make diagonal rows and press.

2. Pin a sashing row to a block row, matching seam intersections, and sew. Use the clipping trick at the seam intersections and continue to press seam allowances toward the sashings. After the rows are sewn together, add corner triangles and press.

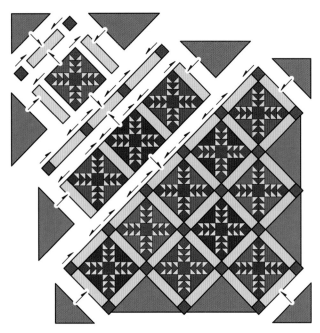

Quilt assembly

3. Trim the edges of the quilt top, leaving a ¼" seam allowance. The outer cornerstones will appear to be halved when sewn. The quilt top should measure 23¼" square, including seam allowances.

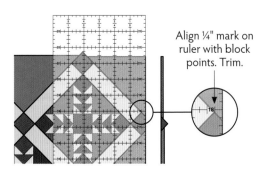

Align ¼" mark on ruler with block points. Trim.

Trim to 23¼" × 23¼".

4. Pin and sew the two brown print 2¾" × 23¼" strips to opposite sides of the quilt top and press. Pin and sew the brown print 2¾" × 27¾" strips to

the top and bottom of the quilt top and press. The quilt top should measure 27¾" square.

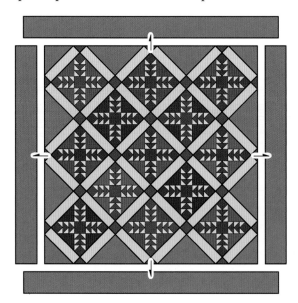

Adding border

Finishing the Quilt

For more detailed information about any finishing steps, visit ShopMartingale.com/HowtoQuilt.

1. Layer the quilt top, batting, and backing. Baste the layers together.

2. Hand or machine quilt as desired. The quilt shown is hand quilted, with each block edge quilted in the ditch. Long rows are quilted along the block edges, across the brown cornerstones, and across the quilt. An X is stitched in the center square of each block, with chevrons quilted in the red triangles about ½" from the geese row. A line is quilted through the middle of each cheddar sashing strip and brown cornerstone. The border and setting triangles are quilted in a crosshatch grid spaced 1" apart.

3. Use the red print 1⅛"-wide strips to make and attach single-fold binding (see "Single-Fold Binding" on page 94).

4. Make and attach a hanging sleeve, if desired.

5. Make, sign, and date a label and attach it to the back of your quilt.

TEA FOR YOU

Materials

Yardage is based on 42"-wide fabric. Fat quarters are 18" × 21"; fat eighths are 9" × 21".

⅜ yard *total* of assorted cream prints for blocks
⅜ yard *total* of assorted brown prints for blocks
1 fat eighth of red print for blocks
1 fat quarter of tan print for blocks
1 fat quarter of teal print for inner border
⅝ yard of brown print for outer border and
   single-fold binding
⅝ yard of fabric for backing
22" × 25" piece of batting

Cutting

From the assorted cream prints, cut:
10 *matching sets* of:
    1 square, 2⅞" × 2⅞" (10 total)
    3 squares, 1⅞" × 1⅞" (30 total)

From the assorted brown prints, cut:
10 *matching sets* of:
    1 square, 2⅞" × 2⅞" (10 total)
    3 squares, 1⅞" × 1⅞" (30 total)

From the red print, cut:
3 strips, 1¼" × 21"; crosscut into 40 squares, 1¼" × 1¼"

From the tan print, cut:
3 strips, 1¼" × 21"; crosscut into 40 squares, 1¼" × 1¼"
2 strips, 2" × 21"; crosscut into 20 squares, 2" × 2"

From the *lengthwise* grain of the teal print, cut:
2 strips, 1" × 15½"
2 strips, 1" × 13½"

From the *lengthwise* grain of the brown print, cut:
2 strips, 2½" × 17½"
2 strips, 2½" × 16½"

From the *crosswise* grain of the remainder of the brown print, cut:
3 strips, 1⅛" × 30"

Color is usually what draws me in, whether we're talking about quilts or antiques. In fact, when I'm attracted to stoneware, like the crocks on the previous page, it's often the yellow and gold undertones that attract my eye, rather than the cool gray ones that are more common.

The 3" T blocks in this quilt are so cute. This is the second T quilt I've made that's been inspired by an antique doll quilt at the International Quilt Study Center & Museum in Lincoln, Nebraska. I added small four-patch units in the alternate blocks to create a chain between the diagonal T block rows.

Finished quilt: 17½" × 20½"
Finished block: 3" × 3"

~

*Pieced by Jo Morton and
quilted by Maggi Honeyman*

Making the T Blocks

The instructions are written to make one block at a time. Press all seam allowances as shown by the arrows in the illustrations.

1. Select the following pieces for one block:
   - 1 matching set of 1 cream print 2⅞" square and 3 cream 1⅞" squares
   - 1 matching set of 1 brown print 2⅞" square and 3 brown print 1⅞" squares

2. Draw a diagonal line from corner to corner on the wrong side of the cream 2⅞" square. Align the marked square with the brown 2⅞" square, right sides together. Sew a scant ¼" from each side of the drawn line. Cut on the drawn line and carefully press to make two half-square-triangle units that measure 2½" square. One is extra.

Make 2 units,
2½" × 2½".

3. Repeat step 2 with the three cream 1⅞" squares and the three brown print 1⅞" squares to make six half-square-triangle units that measure 1½" square. One is extra.

Make 6 units,
1½" × 1½".

4. Lay out the half-square-triangle units to form the T block as shown. Sew into rows and press. Sew the rows together and use the "Clipping Trick" on page 90 to press the block. Make a total of 10 blocks that measure 3½" square, including seam allowances.

Make 10 blocks,
3½" × 3½".

Making the Chain Blocks

1. Sew two tan and two red 1¼" squares together and press to make a four-patch unit that measures 2" square. Make 20 units.

Make 20 units,
2" × 2".

2. Arrange and sew two four-patch units with two tan 2" squares as shown to make a Chain block. Use the clipping trick at the center, press the seam allowances toward the tan squares and press the clipped intersection open. Make 10 blocks that measure 3½" square, including seam allowances.

Make 10 blocks,
3½" × 3½".

~ **pressing details** ~

Press all the blocks in the same manner—it makes the quilting much easier when you have consistent pressing, creating consistent ditches for machine quilting.

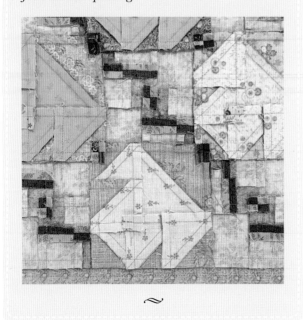

~

~ **clipping trick** ~

Use the "Clipping Trick" on page 90 to press final seam allowances toward the unpieced squares.

~

Assembling the Quilt Top

1. Arrange the T blocks and Chain blocks into five rows of four blocks each, alternating the blocks as shown in the assembly diagram below. Sew the blocks into rows and use the clipping trick at the block intersections to press the seam allowances toward the Chain blocks. Sew the rows together and press. The quilt center should measure 12½" × 15½", including seam allowances.

2. Pin and sew the teal print 1" × 15½" strips to the sides of the quilt top and press. Pin and sew the teal print 1" × 13½" strips to the top and bottom of the quilt top and press.

3. Pin and sew the brown print 2½" × 16½" strips to the sides of the quilt top and press. Pin and sew the brown print 2½" × 17½" strips to the top and bottom of the quilt top and press. The quilt top should measure 17½" × 20½".

Finishing the Quilt

For more detailed information about any finishing steps, visit ShopMartingale.com/HowtoQuilt.

1. Layer the quilt top, batting, and backing. Baste the layers together.

2. Hand or machine quilt as desired. The T blocks are quilted in the ditch and the Chain blocks are quilted on the diagonal with multiple Xs. The inner border is stitched in the ditch, and the outer border continues a diagonal grid pattern.

3. Use the brown print 1⅛"-wide strips to make and attach single-fold binding (see "Single-Fold Binding" on page 94).

4. Make and attach a hanging sleeve, if desired.

5. Make, sign, and date a label and attach it to the back of your quilt.

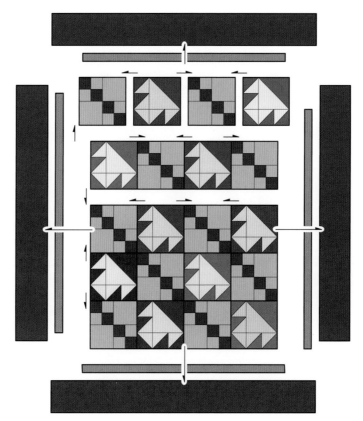

Quilt assembly

BASKET PARADE

D oesn't everyone love baskets and batiks? This quilt gives you the best of both worlds. I used batiks for many of the basket appliqués and in the piecing. The simple basket is easy to stitch, and it complements the center block of swirling leaves and berries. The alternate setting blocks allow you to spotlight a cherished print as well.

Hang the quilt on a wall as a focal point in any room, and use what you have to decorate around it. The wooden bin in our study is a vessel for rotating displays of quilts that shift with the seasons. My featherweight machine isn't tucked away when not in use. Instead, it sits in a place of honor in full view. A few books to peruse from my easy chair are also kept close at hand. What could be better?

Materials

Yardage is based on 42"-wide fabric. Fat quarters are 18" × 21".

⅝ yard of tan print for center block background, flying geese background, and single-fold binding
1 square, 10" × 10", of brown print for leaf appliqués
Scraps of assorted red prints for berry appliqués
1 yard *total* of assorted cream prints for Basket block backgrounds
1 yard *total* of assorted batiks or prints for flying geese and basket appliqués
¾ yard of brown print for Basket block frames
1 fat quarter of brown print for frame of center block
1⅛ yards of red print for two inner borders
⅞ yard of floral for setting squares
⅔ yard of brown batik for setting triangles
1¾ yards of brown stripe for outer border
4 yards of fabric for backing
64" × 64" piece of batting

Cutting

From the tan print, cut:*
6 strips, 1⅛" × 42"
1 square, 11½" × 11½"
56 squares, 1⅞" × 1⅞"

From the assorted cream prints, cut:
32 squares, 5½" × 5½"

From the assorted batiks or prints, cut:
14 squares, 3¼" × 3¼"
32 squares, 4½" × 4½" (for basket appliqués)

From the brown print yardage, cut:
2 strips, 5" × 42"; crosscut into 64 strips, 1" × 5"
2 strips, 6" × 42"; crosscut into 64 strips, 1" × 6"

From the *lengthwise* grain of the brown print fat quarter, cut:
2 strips, 1½" × 10½"
2 strips, 1½" × 12½"

For the most efficient use of your fabric, cut the pieces in the order listed.

Continued on page 50

Finished quilt: 57½" × 57½"
Finished Basket block:
5½" × 5½" framed
Finished Center block: 10" × 10"

~

*Pieced and appliquéd by Jo Morton
and Julie Kiffin
and quilted by Lori Kukuk*

Continued from page 49

From the *lengthwise* grain of the red print, cut:
2 strips, 1" × 16½"
2 strips, 1" × 17½"
6 strips, 1" × 36"

From the floral, cut:
4 strips, 6" × 42"; crosscut into 20 squares, 6" × 6"

From the brown batik, cut:
5 squares, 9½" × 9½"; cut into quarters diagonally to make 20 triangles
2 squares, 5¼" × 5¼"; cut in half diagonally to make 4 triangles

From the *lengthwise* grain of the brown stripe, cut:**
2 strips, 5¼" × 48"
2 strips, 5¼" × 57½"

**I fussy cut the print so that the light stripe was next to the red inner border; consider your stripe to determine where to cut. You may also want to cut the strips a bit wider or narrower, depending on your fabric.

Appliquéing the Blocks

I appliquéd the blocks using my favorite method, back-basting appliqué. If you use this technique, you do not need to create templates or cut the appliqué shapes beforehand. You'll find how-to information for this technique beginning on page 90 and the appliqué patterns on page 55. You can, of course, use your own preferred method of appliqué.

1. Using the pattern for the center block, appliqué the shapes to the tan print 11½" square. After stitching is complete, square the block to measure 10½" × 10½", keeping the appliqué centered.

Make 1 block.
Trim to 10½" × 10½".

2. Using the pattern for the basket, appliqué a batik basket to each of the 32 cream print 5½" squares. After stitching is complete, trim the blocks to measure 5" × 5", keeping the basket centered.

Make 32.
Trim to 5" × 5".

3. Sew brown print 1" × 5" sashing strips to opposite sides of a Basket block and press as indicated by the arrows. Sew brown print 1" × 6" sashing strips to the top and bottom of the block and press. The block should measure 6" square, including seam allowances. Repeat for all 32 Basket blocks.

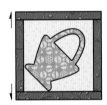

Make 32 blocks,
6" × 6".

Making the Flying Geese

Press all seam allowances as shown by the arrows in the illustrations.

1. Draw a diagonal line from corner to corner on the wrong side of four tan print 1⅞" squares. Align two squares on opposite corners of a print 3¼" square, right sides together. The squares will overlap in the center. Sew a scant ¼" from each side of the drawn lines. Cut on the drawn lines and press.

Make 2 units.

2. Align a tan print 1⅞" square on the corner of one of the large triangles, noting the direction of the diagonal line. Sew a scant ¼" from each side of the

drawn line. Cut on the line and press. Repeat with the remaining unit to make four identical flying-geese units that measure 1½" × 2½". Make 14 sets of four units, for a total of 56.

Make 56 units,
1½" × 2½".

~ take time to trim ~

Patchwork blocks usually have some stray threads, and trimming gets rid of them and the "dog ears" that stick out. Please square up; do not just cut the ears off. It will make the quilt assembly easier. Bloc Loc makes a 1" × 2" finished-size flying-geese ruler that makes the squaring up very quick and easy.

~

Assembling the Quilt Center

1. Pin and sew the brown print 1½" × 10½" strips to opposite sides of the appliquéd center block and press. Pin and sew the brown print 1½" × 12½" strips to the top and bottom of the block and press. The unit should measure 12½" square, including seam allowances; getting the size correct is important or the flying-geese border won't fit. Trim evenly if necessary.

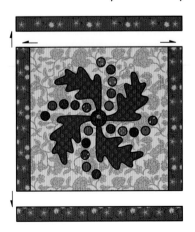

2. Arrange 12 flying-geese units in a row and sew them together to make a side border; press. The border needs to measure 2½" × 12½" to fit the center block. Adjust the seams if necessary. Repeat to make a total of two side borders.

Make 2 side borders, 2½" × 12½".

3. Arrange 14 flying-geese units in a row and sew them together; press. Join two flying-geese units, press, and then sew them to the right-hand end of the longer unit, orienting the points upward as shown. Press. Repeat to make a total of two top/bottom borders. The borders should measure 2½" × 16½"; adjust the seams if necessary.

Make 2 top/bottom borders, 2½" × 16½".

4. Pin and sew the side borders to opposite sides of the quilt center; note that the geese fly in opposite directions. Press. Pin and sew the remaining borders to the top and bottom as shown so that all geese are flying counterclockwise and press. The quilt center should measure 16½" square, including seam allowances. Correct measurements are critical, so adjust seams now if needed.

5. Pin and sew the red 1" × 16½" strips to opposite sides of the quilt center and press. Pin and sew the red 1" × 17½" strips to the top and bottom of the quilt center and press. Evenly trim and square up the quilt center to measure 17" × 17". This measurement is important for quilt-top assembly—there's no room for fudging. After the blocks have been added to the quilt, you'll have a ¼"-wide red accent border.

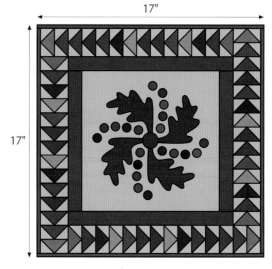

Make 1 center unit.

Assembling the Quilt Top

1. Referring to the photo on page 50 and the quilt assembly diagram below, arrange the framed Basket blocks on point, in six horizontal rows, placing the quilt center on point in the middle. Fill in with the floral 6" setting squares. Add the batik side and corner setting triangles.

2. Pin the blocks into four corner sections and four side sections, matching the seam intersections. Sew the blocks together to complete each section, using the "Clipping Trick" on page 90 at the seam intersections as needed. Press, keeping any clipped intersections open.

3. Sew the upper-right and lower-left corner sections to opposite sides of the quilt center and press.

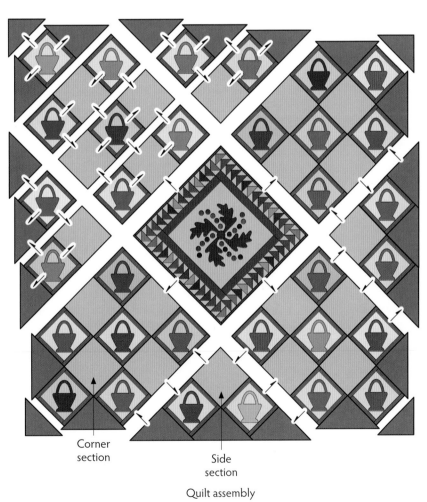

Corner section

Side section

Quilt assembly

4. Pin and sew together the lower-right corner section and two side sections, matching the seam intersections, and press. Repeat with the upper-left corner section and two side sections. Use the clipping trick at the seam intersections to press seam allowances toward the alternate blocks; press the clipped intersections open.

5. Pin and sew the lower-right corner, the quilt center, and the upper-left corner of the quilt together, matching the seam intersections. Use the clipping trick at the seam intersections to press the seam allowances toward the setting squares. Press the clipped intersections open. Add the corner triangles and press. Trim and square up the quilt center to measure 47" × 47".

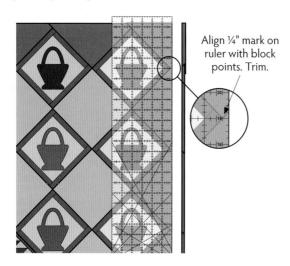

Align ¼" mark on ruler with block points. Trim.

Trim to 47" × 47".

6. Sew the six red 1" × 36" strips together with straight seams to make one long strip. Cut this length into two strips, 1" × 47", and two strips, 1" × 48", for the inner border.

7. Pin and sew the red 1" × 47" strips to opposite sides of the quilt center and press. Pin and sew the red 1" × 48" strips to the top and bottom of the quilt top and press. The quilt top should measure 48" square, including seam allowances.

8. Pin and sew the brown stripe 5¼" × 48" strips to the top and bottom of the quilt and press. Pin and sew the brown stripe 5¼" × 57½" strips to the left

and right sides of the quilt and press. The quilt top should measure 57½" square.

Adding borders

Finishing the Quilt

For more detailed information about any finishing steps, visit ShopMartingale.com/HowtoQuilt.

1. Layer the quilt top, batting, and backing. Baste the layers together.

2. Hand or machine quilt as desired. All the blocks, flying-geese units, framing strips, and the red inner border are quilted in the ditch. The center appliqués and baskets are echo quilted in lines about ¼" apart. Veins are quilted in the leaves of the center block. A curving vine is quilted in the brown print border around it. The basket interiors are echo quilted about ¼" from the basket edge with horizontal lines inside, about ¼" apart, to resemble basket weaving. The setting squares feature a feathered wreath with crosshatching in the center. The setting triangles are quilted with half- and quarter-sections of the feathered wreath. The outer border is crosshatched in lines 1" apart.

3. Use the tan print 1⅛"-wide strips to make and attach single-fold binding (see "Single-Fold Binding" on page 94).

4. Make, sign, and date a label and attach it to the back of your quilt.

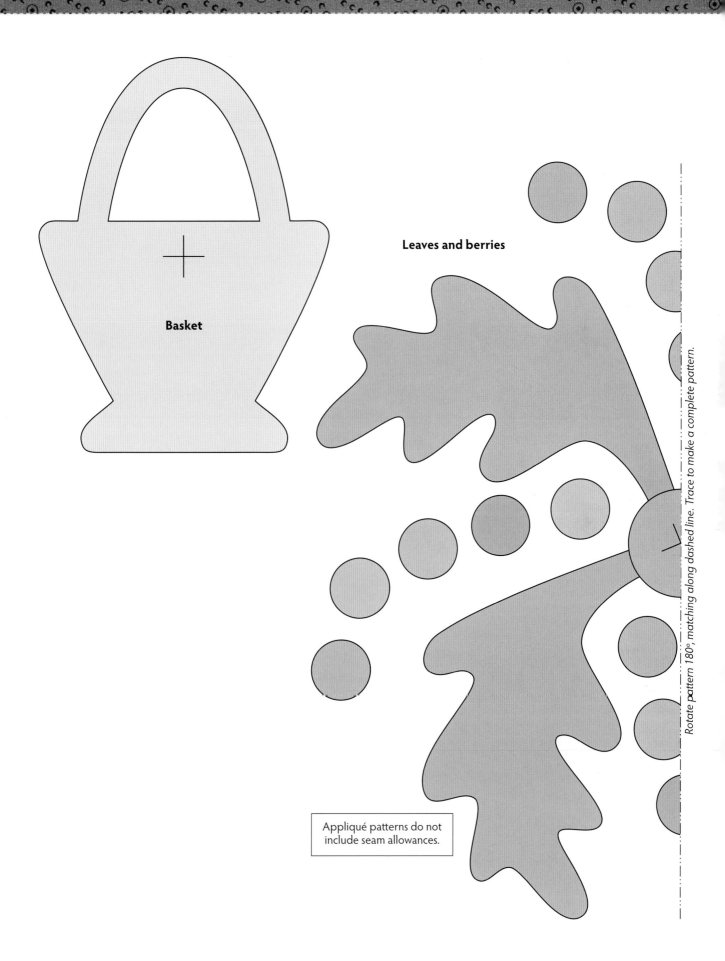

Leaves and berries

Basket

Appliqué patterns do not
include seam allowances.

Rotate pattern 180°, matching along dashed line. Trace to make a complete pattern.

Materials

Yardage is based on 42"-wide fabric. Fat eighths are 9" × 21".

⅜ yard *total* of assorted light prints for blocks
⅜ yard *total* of assorted medium prints for blocks
¼ yard of brown print for setting triangles
⅔ yard of tan print for border
1 fat eighth of brown print for single-fold binding
⅔ yard of fabric for backing
24" × 26" piece of batting

Cutting

From the assorted light prints, cut:
36 squares, 2¾" × 2¾"

From the assorted medium prints, cut:
36 squares, 2¾" × 2¾"

From the brown print yardage, cut:
6 squares, 4¼" × 4¼"; cut into quarters diagonally
    to make 24 triangles (2 are extra)
2 squares, 2½" × 2½"; cut in half diagonally to make
    4 triangles

From the *lengthwise* grain of the tan print, cut:
2 strips, 2½" × 18"
2 strips, 2½" × 19½"

From the brown print fat quarter, cut:
5 strips, 1⅛" × 21"

Making the Blocks

Press all seam allowances as shown by the arrows in the illustrations.

1. Pair a light print 2¾" square with a medium print 2¾" square. Draw a diagonal line from corner to corner on the wrong side of the light square. Align the squares with right sides together and sew a scant ¼" from each side of the drawn line. Cut on the line and press to make two identical half-square-triangle blocks.

This sweet quilt is another that was inspired by an antique bed-sized quilt. Since I have enough bed quilts, I once again made a small quilt that achieves the purpose of owning my own version of an antique quilt.

Obvious pairings are with an antique doll bed or cradle, which makes for a great little display piece. Make this quilt for your daughter or granddaughter to play with. Or, better yet, teach her to make one herself. We want this tradition to continue!

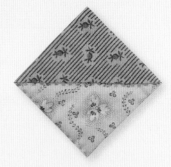

Finished quilt: 19½" × 22"
Finished block: 1¾" × 1¾"

~

Pieced and quilted by Jo Morton

2. Trim the blocks to measure 2¼" square, including seam allowances. Make 72 blocks.

Make 72 blocks.

Assembling the Quilt Top

1. Arrange the blocks on point in seven rows of six blocks each. Fill in with the remaining blocks. Make sure all the lights are pointing downward.

2. Arrange the brown print 4¼" triangles along the sides. Place the four 2½" triangles in the corners. Sew the blocks together in diagonal rows; press seam allowances in opposite directions from row to row.

3. Join the rows, pinning and matching seam intersections. Press the seam allowances open. The setting triangles were cut slightly oversized,

so you will need to trim the edges of the quilt top. Trim the top to measure 15½" × 18", including seam allowances.

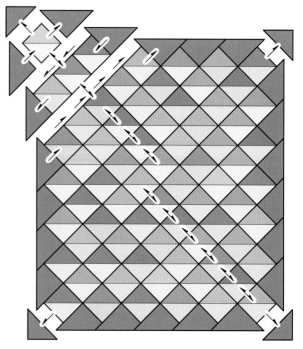

Quilt assembly

4. Pin and sew the tan 2½" × 18" strips to the sides of the quilt top and press. Pin and sew the tan 2½" × 19½" strips to the top and bottom of the quilt; press. The quilt top should measure 19½" × 22".

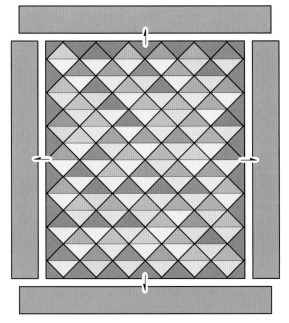

Adding border

Finishing the Quilt

For more detailed information about any finishing steps, visit ShopMartingale.com/HowtoQuilt.

1. Layer the quilt top, batting, and backing. Baste the layers together.

2. Hand or machine quilt as desired. In the quilt shown, light tan thread is used to hand quilt in a diagonal line in the ditch along the diagonal line formed by the rows pressed in opposite directions. The ditch moved back and forth along the diagonal because of the seam-allowance pressing, but it worked. The row seam allowances are pressed open, so I didn't quilt in the opposite direction; I quilted in the ditch along the horizontal lines that were formed by pressing the block seam allowances toward the medium print fabric. The quilting lines extend into the borders.

∾ treasured scraps ∾

Hang onto small pieces left over from your quiltmaking and sort them into small bins of lights, mediums, and darks. (Maybe you need bigger bins—I won't tell on you!) Leftovers are perfect for making this small treasure. Just add a border. This little sweetie is a good size for practicing hand quilting too.

∾

3. Use the brown print 1⅛"-wide strips to make and attach single-fold binding (see "Single-Fold Binding" on page 94).

4. Make and attach a hanging sleeve, if desired.

5. Make, sign, and date a label and attach it to the back of your quilt.

STAR STRIP

Add flair to a side table with this appealing quilt of stars and stripes. The green and gold prints with accents of red make an eye-catching focal point and add a touch of soft texture when placed on wood furniture such as a table, sideboard, or jelly cupboard.

Quilts can keep your favorite tabletops from becoming scratched if the table is where you usually set down sewing supplies such as scissors, hoops, or templates.

I made the Star blocks first and years later pulled them out to go with the green stripe. I think of this quilt and many others as time travelers. They'll be done when they're done.

Materials

Yardage is based on 42"-wide fabric. Fat quarters are 18" × 21".

¼ yard *total* of assorted green prints for blocks
¼ yard *total* of assorted cream prints for blocks
⅛ yard *total* of assorted red, tan, and cheddar prints for blocks
1 fat quarter of cheddar print for block sashing and single-fold binding
1 fat quarter of green stripe for row sashing
1 fat quarter of green-and-gold stripe for border
⅝ yard of fabric for backing
18" × 23" piece of batting

Cutting

From the assorted green prints, cut:
15 *matching sets* of 4 squares, 1½" × 1½" (60 total)

From the assorted cream prints, cut:
15 *matching sets* of:
    4 squares, 1⅛" × 1⅛" (60 total)
    1 square, 2½" × 2½" (15 total)

From the assorted red, tan, and cheddar prints, cut:
15 squares, 1¾" × 1¾"

From the cheddar print fat quarter, cut:
1 strip, 3" × 21"; crosscut into 12 rectangles, 1" × 3"
4 strips, 1⅛" × 21"

From the *lengthwise* grain of the green stripe, cut:*
2 strips, 1¼" × 15"

From the *lengthwise* grain of the green-and-gold stripe, cut:*
2 strips, 2½" × 15"
2 strips, 2½" × 13½"

*You may want to fussy cut these strips, as I did, to center the motifs.

Finished quilt: 13½" × 19"
Finished block: 2½" × 2½"

~

*Pieced and quilted
by Jo Morton*

Making the Blocks

The instructions are written to make one block at a time. Press all seam allowances as shown by the arrows in the illustrations.

1. Select the following for one block:
   - 1 matching set of 4 green print 1½" squares for the star points
   - 1 print 1¾" square for the block center
   - 1 matching set of 1 cream 2½" square and 4 cream 1⅛" squares

2. Draw a diagonal line from corner to corner on the wrong side of the four green print 1½" squares. Align two marked squares on opposite corners of the cream 2½" square, with right sides together. The squares will overlap in the center. Sew a scant ¼" from each side of the drawn lines. Cut on the drawn lines and press.

Make 2 units.

3. Align a green 1½" square on the corner of a cream triangle, noting the direction of the diagonal line. Sew a scant ¼" from each side of the drawn line. Cut on the line and press. Repeat with the second unit to make four matching flying-geese units that measure 1⅛" × 1¾".

Make 4 units,
1⅛" × 1¾".

4. Arrange and sew the flying-geese units, four cream 1⅛" squares, and one print 1¾" square in rows as shown; press. Join the rows to make a block that measures 3" square, including seam allowances. Use the "Clipping Trick" on page 63 at the seam intersections. Make 15 Star blocks.

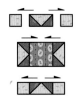

Make 15 blocks,
3" × 3".

～ clipping trick ～

Clip seam allowances to press the flying-geese units toward the center, press the squares toward the corners, and press the seam intersections open.

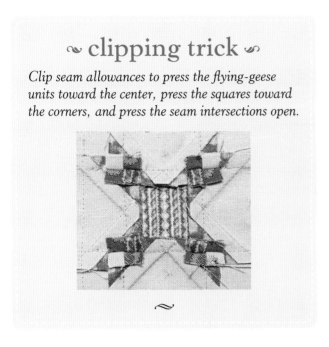

～

Assembling the Quilt Top

1. Referring to the assembly diagram below, sew five blocks and four cheddar print 1" × 3" sashing rectangles in rows and press. Make three rows that measure 3" × 15", including seam allowances.

2. Sew the pieced rows together with the green stripe 1¼" × 15" sashing strips and green-and-gold 2½" × 15" border strips as shown. Press the seam allowances away from the pieced rows. Measure the rows and adjust seam allowances if needed so they match the length of the sashing and borders.

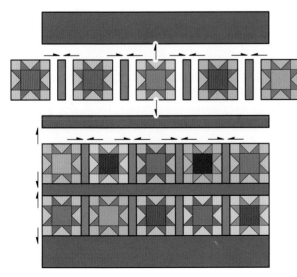

Quilt assembly

3. Sew the green-and-gold 2½" × 13½" strips to the short edges of the quilt. Press.

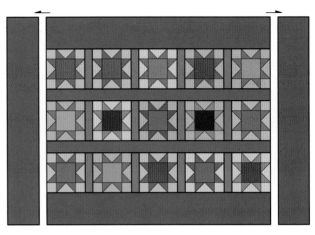

Adding side borders

Finishing the Quilt

For more detailed information about any finishing steps, visit ShopMartingale.com/HowtoQuilt.

1. Layer the quilt top, batting, and backing. Baste the layers together.

2. Hand or machine quilt as desired. The quilt is machine quilted from edge to edge in an uneven crosshatch design. I established a diagonal by using the diagonal lines of the star points. I like simple, traditional quilting on these types of quilts; it allows the graphic design of the quilt to shine.

3. Use the cheddar print 1⅛"-wide strips to make and attach single-fold binding (see "Single-Fold Binding" on page 94).

4. Make and attach a hanging sleeve, if desired.

5. Make, sign, and date a label and attach it to the back of your quilt.

NINE PATCH CHAIN

Materials

Fat quarters are 18" × 21"; fat eighths are 9" × 21".

1 fat quarter of cream print for blocks
1 fat quarter of rust print for blocks
1 fat quarter of brown print for blocks
1 fat eighth of rust print for binding
1 fat quarter of fabric for backing
17" × 17" piece of batting

Cutting

From the *lengthwise* grain of the cream print, cut:
12 strips, 1¼" × 18"

From the *lengthwise* grain of the rust print, cut:
7 strips, 1¼" × 18"

From the *lengthwise* grain of the brown print, cut:
14 strips, 1¼" × 18"

From the rust print fat eighth, cut:
4 strips, 1⅛" × 21"

Making the Blocks

Press all seam allowances as shown by the arrows in the illustrations.

1. Arrange and sew one cream and two brown 1¼" × 18" strips together as shown. Make two strip sets. Cut into 25 segments, 1¼" wide.

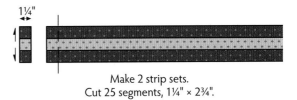

Make 2 strip sets.
Cut 25 segments, 1¼" × 2¾".

2. Arrange and sew one brown and two cream 1¼" × 18" strips together as shown. Make four strip sets. Cut into 50 segments, 1¼" wide.

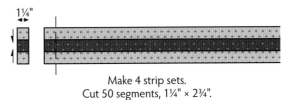

Make 4 strip sets.
Cut 50 segments, 1¼" × 2¾".

An antique quilt made in pinks and greens inspired this petite brown-and-rust version. This quilt is less scrappy than most, but it's fun to choose your three fabrics. Select a dark, medium, and light to best see the chain effect. Drape the quilt in a cupboard or on a shelf. Add dashes of charm with whatever you love to display—old sewing notions, favorite fabric bundles, or wooden spools.

When I travel, I try to collect only small things that will fit into my suitcase as mementos of places I visit. I began collecting crystal salt cellars and toothpick holders. I wanted a pincushion collection, so a friend helped me turn those items into little pincushions. When I see them nestled in a display, warm memories come to mind.

Finished quilt: 13¼" × 13¼"
Finished block: 2¼" × 2¼"

∼

*Pieced by Jo Morton and
quilted by Maggi Honeyman*

3. Join the segments as shown and press to make a Nine Patch block that measures 2¾" square, including seam allowances. Make 25.

Make 25 blocks,
2¾" × 2¾".

4. Arrange and sew one cream and two rust 1¼" × 18" strips as shown. Press. Make two strip sets. Cut into 16 segments, 1¼" wide.

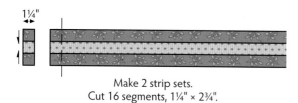

Make 2 strip sets.
Cut 16 segments, 1¼" × 2¾".

5. Arrange and sew one rust and two brown 1¼" × 18" strips as shown. Press. Make three strip sets. Cut into 32 segments, 1¼" wide.

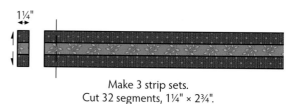

Make 3 strip sets.
Cut 32 segments, 1¼" × 2¾".

6. Join segments as shown and press to make a Nine Patch block that measures 2¾" square, including seam allowances. Make 16.

Make 16 blocks,
2¾" × 2¾".

Assembling the Quilt Top

1. Arrange the blocks on point, alternating them as shown. Sew them in diagonal rows and press.

2. Pin the rows together, matching seam intersections, and sew. Press carefully.

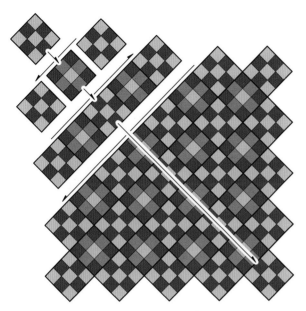

Quilt assembly

3. Trim and square up the quilt top, leaving a ¼" seam allowance all around. The lines on your ruler are very helpful for centering and leaving the seam allowance. The quilt top should measure approximately 13¼" square.

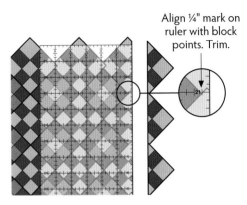

Align ¼" mark on ruler with block points. Trim.

Trim to 13¼" × 13¼".

Finishing the Quilt

For more detailed information about any finishing steps, visit ShopMartingale.com/HowtoQuilt.

1. Layer the quilt top, batting, and backing. Baste the layers together.

2. Hand or machine quilt as desired. The quilt shown is machine quilted in an allover meander pattern.

3. Use the rust print 1⅛"-wide strips to make and attach single-fold binding (see "Single-Fold Binding" on page 94).

4. Make and attach a hanging sleeve, if desired.

5. Make, sign, and date a label and attach it to the back of your quilt.

BLOOM

The sweet, small Four Patch blocks in this quilt provide an ideal destination for tiny scraps that don't have a place to go. I like scrappy Four Patches, where the stripes can run in different directions and the combinations aren't dictated by sewing strips together and subcutting multiple units from the same fabrics. Perhaps it's old-fashioned, but what a perfect way to use up bits and pieces. I set my blocks with pink and brown, a traditional favorite. You can hang this quilt on the wall above a treasured piece of furniture or add an accent of something old and something new.

Materials

Yardage is based on 42"-wide fabric. Fat quarters are 18" × 21".

⅓ yard *total* of assorted brown, blue, red, and gold prints for blocks
⅓ yard *total* of assorted light prints for blocks
½ yard of pink print for blocks and single-fold binding
1 fat quarter of cream print for setting squares
¾ yard of brown stripe for border
⅛ yard of brown print for border cornerstones
1 yard of fabric for backing
32" × 32" piece of batting

Cutting

From the assorted light prints, cut:
104 squares, 1¼" × 1¼"

From the assorted brown, blue, red, and gold prints, cut:
104 squares, 1¼" × 1¼"

From the pink print, cut:
2 strips, 2" × 42"; crosscut into 39 squares, 2" × 2". Cut 26 squares in half diagonally to yield 52 triangles.
2 strips, 3½" × 42"; crosscut into 13 squares, 3½" × 3½". Cut into quarters diagonally to yield 52 triangles.
3 strips, 1⅛" × 42"

From the cream print, cut:
12 squares, 4¾" × 4¾"

From the *lengthwise* grain of the brown stripe, fussy cut:
4 strips, 3½" × 21¾"

From the brown print, cut:
4 squares, 3½" × 3½"

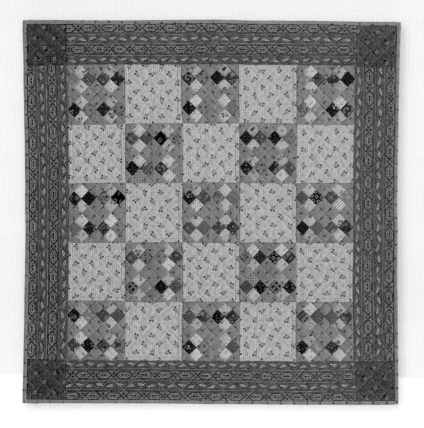

Finished quilt: 27¾" × 27¾"
Finished four-patch unit: 1½" × 1½"
Finished block: 4¼" × 4¼"

*Pieced by Jo Morton and quilted
by Maggi Honeyman*

Making the Blocks

Press all seam allowances as shown by the arrows in the illustrations.

1. Select two light 1¼" squares and two brown, blue, red, or gold 1¼" squares; they can be matching or different. Sew each light square to a darker square and press. Align two of these units, matching the seam intersections, and sew to make a four-patch unit. Press. Make 52 units that measure 2" square, including seam allowances.

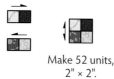

Make 52 units,
2" × 2".

2. Arrange four of the four-patch units, a pink 2" square, four pink 3½" side triangles, and four pink 2" corner triangles together as shown with the dark squares running horizontally. Sew the units into diagonal rows and press. Pin the rows together, matching seam intersections, and sew. Use the "Clipping Trick" on page 90 at the seam

intersections. Continue to press seam allowances toward the pink fabric and press the clipped intersections open.

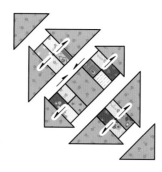

3. Trim and square the block to measure 4¾" square, including seam allowances. Make 13.

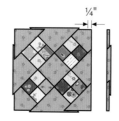

¼"

Make 13 blocks,
4¾" × 4¾".

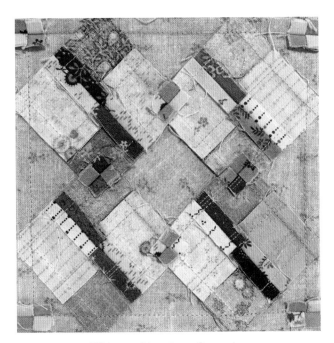

This combination of pressing helps blocks lie nice and flat.

Assembling the Quilt Top

1. Arrange the blocks and setting squares into five rows as shown in the assembly diagram, above right, alternating the pieced blocks and setting squares. Sew the blocks into rows and press. Pin and sew the rows together in groups of two. Use the clipping trick at the seam intersections; continue to press the seam allowances toward the light print squares, and press the clipped intersections open. Continue to sew the rest of the rows together. The quilt top should measure 21¾" square, including seam allowances.

2. Pin and sew brown stripe 3½" × 21¾" strips to opposite sides of the quilt and press.

3. Sew the brown print 3½" cornerstones to the ends of the two remaining border strips and press. Pin the borders to the top and bottom of the quilt, matching seam intersections, and sew. Use the clipping trick at the seam intersections. Press the

seam allowances toward the border, and press the clipped intersections open. The quilt top should measure 27¾" square.

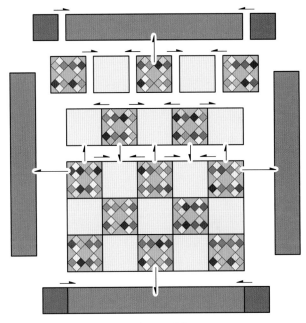

Quilt assembly

Finishing the Quilt

For more detailed information about any finishing steps, visit ShopMartingale.com/HowtoQuilt.

1. Layer the quilt top, batting, and backing. Baste the layers together.

2. Hand or machine quilt as desired. The quilt shown features a crosshatch grid based on the pieced blocks. The grid extends into the border. The setting squares are outline quilted and filled with a squared-off feathered wreath design.

3. Use the pink print 1⅛"-wide strips to make and attach single-fold binding (see "Single-Fold Binding" on page 94).

4. Make and attach a hanging sleeve, if desired.

5. Make, sign, and date a label and attach it to the back of your quilt.

WINSLOW ALLEY

Materials

Yardage is based on 42"-wide fabric. Fat quarters are 18" × 21".

⅜ yard *total* of assorted brown prints for blocks
⅜ yard *total* of assorted cream prints for blocks
1 fat quarter of cheddar print for setting triangles
⅞ yard of paisley print for sashing strips
⅞ yard of eggplant print for border
¼ yard of green stripe for single-fold binding
¾ yard of fabric for backing
23" × 32" piece of batting

Cutting

From the assorted brown prints, cut:*
14 squares, 4½" × 4½"

From the assorted cream prints, cut:*
14 squares, 4½" × 4½"

From the cheddar print, cut:
12 squares, 4¼" × 4¼"; cut into quarters diagonally to make 48 triangles
6 squares, 2½" × 2½"; cut in half diagonally to make 12 triangles

From the *lengthwise* grain of the paisley print, cut:**
2 strips, 2¼" × 26"

From the *lengthwise* grain of the eggplant print, cut:**
2 strips, 3½" × 26"
2 strips, 1½" × 18⅝"

From the green stripe, cut:
3 strips, 1⅛" × 42"

*For scrappier blocks, cut 54 brown print 2" squares and 54 cream print 2" squares instead of fewer 4½" squares.

**I suggest waiting until you measure the block columns to cut them to the length needed.

A quilt doesn't always have to be the center of attention. Redware pottery pieces with their squiggly lines and rich colors are the showstoppers in my dining room, but their colors complement this graphic vertical quilt nicely.

There's something about strippy quilts that I just love. Maybe it's because you can give favorite fabrics such prominent placement while still enjoying the fun of piecing little blocks.

Finished quilt: 18⅝" × 28"
Finished block: 2" × 2"

~

*Pieced by Jo Morton and
quilted by Maggi Honeyman*

Making the Blocks

Press all seam allowances as shown by the arrows in the illustrations.

1. Pair a brown print 4½" square with a cream print 4½" square. Draw a diagonal line from corner to corner in each direction on the wrong side of the cream square to make an X. Layer the squares right sides together. (If you have chosen to make scrappier blocks, draw one diagonal line from corner to corner on the wrong side of the cream 2" squares.)

2. Sew with a scant ¼" seam on both sides of the diagonal lines. Cut the squares in half vertically and horizontally on the 2¼" center. Then cut the units on the diagonal lines, and press to make eight identical half-square-triangle units. Trim

and square the units to measure 1½" × 1½". Make a total of 112; four will be extra. (For scrappy blocks, cut the 2" squares on the diagonal line, press, and trim to make two identical units. Make a total of 108.)

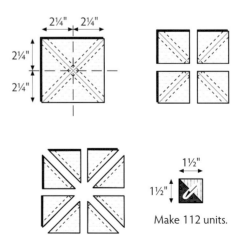

Make 112 units.

～ making half-square-triangle units ～

I have two favorite methods of making half-square-triangle units. The first method is to make slightly oversized units by layering two squares together, drawing a diagonal line (or lines) from corner to corner, sewing, and cutting. I then use a Bloc Loc ruler for trimming. They come in several sizes; my favorite is the 3½" or the 4½". I use this to square up any units that are smaller than the ruler. There is a groove on the underside of the ruler that allows you to snug the ruler up against the diagonal seam, trim two sides, rotate, and then trim the remaining two sides.

The second method is to use triangle foundation paper. It comes in many sizes and is reasonably priced. I subcut a large sheet into segments that will make eight half-square-triangle units at a time. Simply layer two fabric squares right sides together with the paper foundation printed side up on top of the lighter square. Sew on the dotted lines using a 1.5 stitch length (about 18 stitches per inch), and then cut on the solid lines using a rotary cutter and ruler. Leaving the paper attached, press the diagonal seam toward the dark fabric. I remove the papers while watching TV and trim the little fabric tips with scissors. They are ready to use with no squaring up. Leaving the paper in place while pressing stabilizes the unit and prevents distortion.

I used 1" triangle paper to make the half-square-triangle units for this quilt. The instructions are written for the first method to make eight identical units at once.

3. Arrange four of the half-square-triangle units as shown; all the cream prints should be going in the same direction. Sew the units together in pairs and press; sew the pairs together and press. Use the "Clipping Trick" on page 90 at the seam intersection, and press the seam allowances in opposite directions. Press the clipped intersection open. Make a total of 27 blocks that measure 2½" square, including seam allowances.

Make 27 blocks,
2½" × 2½".

Assembling the Quilt Top

1. Arrange the blocks into three vertical rows of nine blocks each; note that the blocks in the middle row have the dark triangles pointing upward. Add the cheddar print setting triangles. Since my cheddar print is a subtle stripe, I alternated the direction of the stripe in every other pair of setting triangles. This will depend on your fabric. I arranged everything on my design wall before sewing the blocks and triangles together.

2. Sew the blocks and side setting triangles into diagonal rows and press. Pin and sew the diagonal rows together, matching seam intersections. Use the clipping trick at the intersections and press the seam allowances toward the setting triangles. Press the clipped

intersections open. Sew the corner triangles last and press. Make three rows.

Make 1 row.   Make 2 rows.

3. Trim away the excess fabric, leaving the ¼" seam allowance. Be very careful when pressing the vertical rows, or they may "grow." All three rows need to be the same length. The rows should measure 3⅜" × 26", including seam allowances, after trimming. Adjust the length of sashing and border strips if your measurements differ from that.

4. Arrange the three pieced rows with the two paisley 2¼" × 26" sashing strips. Note the orientation of the blocks and make sure the rows are correct before sewing. Pin and sew the sashing strips and rows together and press. The top should measure 12⅝" × 26", including seam allowances.

5. Pin and sew the eggplant 3½" × 26" strips to the sides of your quilt top and press. Pin and sew the eggplant 1½" × 18⅝" strips to the top and bottom and press. The top should measure 18⅝" × 28".

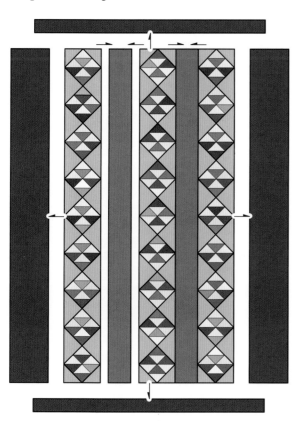

Quilt assembly

Finishing the Quilt

For more detailed information about any finishing steps, visit ShopMartingale.com/HowtoQuilt.

1. Layer the quilt top, batting, and backing. Baste the layers together.

2. Hand or machine quilt as desired. The quilt shown is stitched in an overall, edge-to-edge diagonal grid, based on the squares in the pieced blocks.

3. Use the green stripe 1⅛"-wide strips to make and attach single-fold binding (see "Single-Fold Binding" on page 94).

4. Make and attach a hanging sleeve, if desired.

5. Make, sign, and date a label and attach it to the back of your quilt.

TIC-TAC-TOE

Materials

Yardage is based on 42"-wide fabric.

⅓ yard *total* of assorted brown A prints for blocks

⅝ yard *total* of assorted pink prints for blocks and Sawtooth border

⅝ yard of light print for blocks and Sawtooth border

¼ yard of blue print for blocks and cornerstones

¼ yard of gold print for blocks

¾ yard of brown B print for setting squares, triangles, and binding

1 yard of pink floral for outer border

1¼ yards of fabric for backing

41" × 41" piece of batting

Cutting

Each block contains light, blue, and gold fabrics, along with a variety of either brown or pink fabrics. Repeat the cutting instructions to make 5 brown blocks and 4 pink blocks (9 blocks total).

FOR 1 BLOCK

From the assorted brown A or pink prints, cut:
16 squares, 1½" × 1½"

From the light print, cut:
16 squares, 1½" × 1½"

From the blue print, cut:
4 squares, 1½" × 1½"
1 square, 1" × 1"

From the gold print, cut:
4 rectangles, 1" × 3½"

FOR THE SAWTOOTH BORDER

From the light print, cut:
12 squares, 4½" × 4½"

From the assorted pink prints, cut:
12 squares, 4½" × 4½"

Continued on page 80

ost of my quilts begin with making a few blocks and then playing with them; this one began with the 3" Nine Patches. I began piecing these blocks at a retreat and I thought they were cute! But they looked ordinary with an alternate 3" setting fabric, so the challenge to spotlight them began. Anyway, long story short, the Nine Patches look delightful with the narrow sashing between them.

I paired this quilt with a wicker laundry basket because I like how the weave of the wicker plays so nicely with the lattice effect in the patchwork blocks. Rounding out this vignette are some favorite French-themed treasures, as France is one of my favorite places to visit.

Finished quilt: 36½" × 36½"
Finished block: 6½" × 6½"

~

*Pieced and quilted
by Jo Morton*

Continued from page 79

FOR THE SETTING SQUARES AND TRIANGLES

From the brown B print, cut:

2 squares, 11" × 11"; cut the squares into quarters diagonally to yield 8 setting triangles

2 squares, 6" × 6"; cut the squares in half diagonally to yield 4 corner triangles

4 squares, 7" × 7"

FOR THE OUTER BORDER, CORNERSTONES, AND BINDING

From the *lengthwise* grain of the pink floral, cut:

4 strips, 3½" × 30½"

From the blue print, cut:

4 squares, 3½" × 3½"

From the brown B print, cut:

4 strips, 1⅛" × 42", for binding

Making the Blocks

Press all seam allowances as shown by the arrows in the illustrations.

1. Lay out four brown A squares, four light squares, and one blue 1½" square in three rows as shown. Sew the squares together into rows. Join the rows to complete a nine-patch unit measuring 3½" square. Use the "Clipping Trick" on page 90 at the seam intersections to press the seam allowances toward the brown and blue squares; press the clipped intersections open. Make a total of 20 nine-patch units.

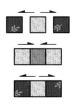

Make 20 units,
3½" × 3½".

2. Repeat step 1 using four pink squares, four light squares, and one blue 1½" square to make 16 nine-patch units.

Make 16 units,
3½" × 3½".

3. Lay out four brown A nine-patch units, four gold 1" × 3½" rectangles, and one blue 1" square in three rows as shown. Sew the pieces together into rows. Join the rows to make a block measuring 7" square. Make a total of five blocks.

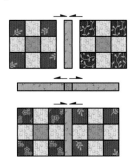

Make 5 blocks,
7" × 7".

4. Lay out four pink nine-patch units, four gold 1" × 3½" rectangles, and one blue 1" square in three rows as shown. Sew the pieces together into rows. Join the rows to make a block measuring 7" square. Make a total of four blocks.

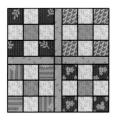

Make 4 blocks,
7" × 7".

Making the Sawtooth Border

1. Draw a diagonal line from corner to corner in both directions on the wrong side of each light 4½" square.

2. Lay a marked light square on top of a pink 4½" square, right sides together. Sew a scant ¼" from each side of the drawn lines.

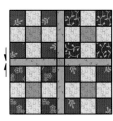

3. Cut the sewn squares apart *first* horizontally and then vertically to make four segments.

4. Cut each segment apart on the drawn diagonal line to make eight half-square-triangle units (each segment yields two half-square-triangle units). Trim each unit to measure 1¾" square. Make a total of 96 units. (You'll use 92.)

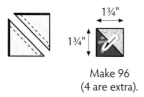

Make 96
(4 are extra).

5. Sew 22 half-square-triangle units together as shown to make a 28"-long side border strip. Press the seam allowances open to reduce bulk. Repeat to make a second side border strip.

Make 2 side borders.

6. Sew 24 half-square-triangle units together as shown to make a 30½"-long top border strip. Press the seam allowances open to reduce bulk. Repeat to make a bottom border strip.

Make 2 top/bottom borders.

Assembling the Quilt Top

1. Lay out the blocks and brown B setting squares with the brown B side and corner triangles in diagonal rows as shown. Sew the pieces together into rows. Join the rows, matching the seam intersections. Add the corner triangles last. Use the clipping trick at the seam intersections to press the seam allowances toward the brown B squares

and triangles; press the clipped intersections open. Trim and square up the quilt top to measure 28" square, including seam allowances, making sure to leave a ¼" seam allowance beyond all points.

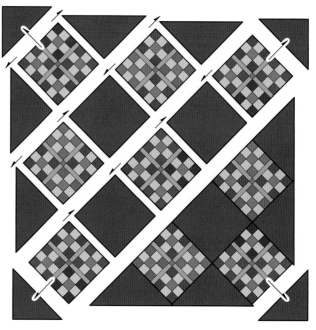

Quilt assembly

2. Sew the 28"-long Sawtooth border strips to opposite sides of the quilt top with the pink prints adjoining the quilt center as shown in the diagram on page 83. Sew the 30½"-long Sawtooth border strips to the top and bottom of the quilt top. The quilt top should measure 30½" square, including seam allowances.

3. Sew the pink floral 30½"-long strips to opposite sides of the quilt top. Sew a blue 3½" square to the ends of each remaining pink floral 30½"-long strip. Sew these strips to the top and bottom of the quilt top. The quilt top should measure 36½" square.

❧ making the borders fit ❧

If the Sawtooth border isn't a perfect fit, you'll need to adjust the seam allowances in a few places. To make the strip slightly longer, make a narrower seam allowance. If the border is a little too long, make a wider seam allowance. Be sure to spread the adjustments across the entire border and it will work out just fine.

Finishing the Quilt

For more detailed information about any finishing steps, visit ShopMartingale.com/HowtoQuilt.

1. Layer the quilt top, batting, and backing. Baste the layers together.

2. Hand or machine quilt as desired. The quilt shown is machine quilted in the ditch. A squared double-feather wreath is quilted in the setting squares and a half-square feather wreath is quilted in the side triangles. The two borders are treated as one and quilted in a crosshatch design, with the spacing determined by the Sawtooth border.

3. Use the brown 1⅛"-wide strips to make and attach single-fold binding (see "Single-Fold Binding" on page 94).

4. Make and attach a hanging sleeve, if desired.

5. Make, sign, and date a label and attach it to your quilt.

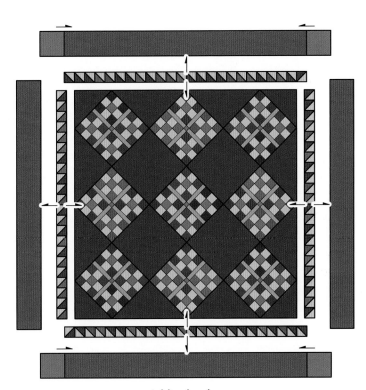

Adding borders

BLUEBERRY MUFFINS

Materials

Yardage is based on 42"-wide fabric. Fat eighths are 9" × 21".

¼ yard *total* of assorted blue prints for blocks
⅓ yard *total* of assorted cream prints for blocks
⅓ yard of brown print for setting triangles
⅔ yard of beige print for sashing and border
1 fat eighth of blue print for single-fold binding
⅝ yard of fabric for backing
21" × 28" piece of batting

Cutting

From the assorted blue prints, cut:
18 *matching sets* of:
    2 squares, 1¾" × 1¾" (36 total)
    1 square, 1¼" × 1¼" (18 total)

From the assorted cream prints, cut:
18 *matching sets* of:
    2 squares, 1¾" × 1¾" (36 total)
    4 squares, 1¼" × 1¼" (72 total)

From the brown print, cut:
8 squares, 4¾" × 4¾"; cut into quarters diagonally to
    make 32 triangles (2 are extra)
6 squares, 2¾" × 2¾"; cut in half diagonally to make
    12 triangles

From the *lengthwise* grain of the beige print, cut:*
2 strips, 2" × 20"
4 strips, 2½" × 20"

From the blue print fat eighth, cut:
5 strips, 1⅛" × 21"

*The beige print border and sashing strips are cut slightly longer than needed. You will trim them to the exact lengths needed after assembling the block rows.

Blue is probably the color most often chosen as a favorite, and it's widely used in decorating schemes. I had fun playing with blue and brown—another favorite of quiltmakers—in this quilt.

"Let's go sew" is my mantra, so I keep these words in plain sight in my sewing studio. When I'm surrounded by the sewing treasures I love, my little quilts, and special gifts from sewing friends, I'm reminded of how fortunate we all are to do what we enjoy. All these things inspire me to keep creating.

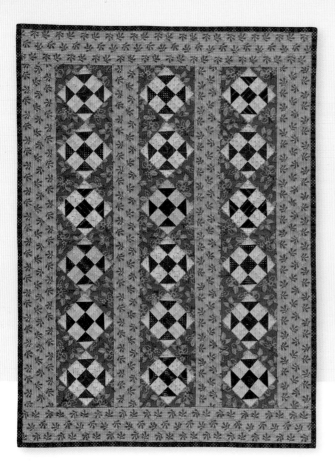

Finished quilt: 17" × 23½"
Finished block: 2¼" × 2¼"

~

Pieced and hand quilted
by Jo Morton

Making the Blocks

The directions are written to make one block at a time. Press all seam allowances as shown by the arrows in the illustrations.

1. Select the following pieces for one block:
   - 1 matching set of 2 blue print 1¾" squares and 1 blue print 1¼" square
   - 1 matching set of 2 cream print 1¾" squares and 4 cream print 1¼" squares

2. Draw a line from corner to corner on the wrong sides of the two cream 1¾" squares. Align each marked square on a blue 1¾" square, right sides together. Sew a scant ¼" from each side of the lines. Cut on the lines; press to make four half-square-triangle units. Trim each to 1¼" square.

Make 4 units.

3. Arrange the half-square-triangle units with the four cream print 1¼" squares and one blue print 1¼" square as shown. Sew into three rows and press. Join the rows. Use the "Clipping Trick" on page 90 at the seam intersections to press seam allowances toward the cream print. The block should measure 2¾" square, including seam allowances. Make a total of 18 blocks.

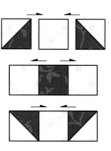 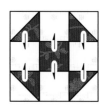

Make 18 blocks, 2¾" × 2¾".

Assembling the Quilt Top

1. Arrange the blocks and setting triangles in three vertical rows of six blocks each as shown. Sew the blocks and triangles together to make diagonal rows, and press. Join the rows, matching seam intersections. Use the clipping trick at the seam intersections so you can continue to press seam allowances toward the brown triangles.

2. Carefully trim the edges ¼" from the block points, as the setting triangles were cut slightly oversize.

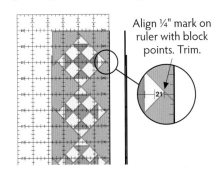

Align ¼" mark on ruler with block points. Trim.

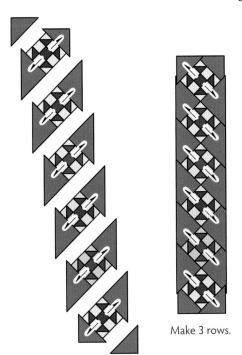

Make 3 rows.

By clipping into the seam allowances, you can press them nice and flat.

3. Measure the length of the pieced rows to determine the length to cut the sashing and borders. Cut two beige print 2"-wide strips for the sashing and cut two beige print 2½"-wide strips for the side borders.

4. Sew the rows together with the sashing strips and the side borders and press.

5. Measure the width of the quilt to determine the length to cut the top and bottom borders. Cut two beige print 2½"-wide strips to this length, and sew them to the top and bottom of the quilt. Press.

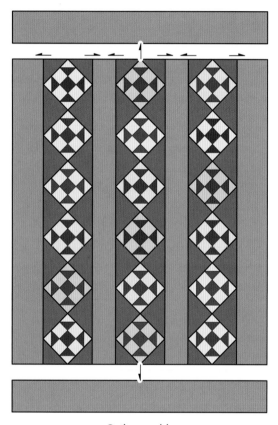

Quilt assembly

Finishing the Quilt

For more detailed information about any finishing steps, visit ShopMartingale.com/HowtoQuilt.

1. Layer the quilt top, batting, and backing. Baste the layers together.

2. Hand or machine quilt as desired. I hand quilted this quilt in a crosshatch design from edge to edge. The spacing was determined by the pieced blocks—I quilted in the ditch of the blocks and then continued across the sashing, through the center of a block, across a sashing along the edge of another block, and then across the borders to the edge. This created lines approximately 1⅛" apart across the quilt.

3. Use the blue print 1⅛"-wide strips to make and attach single-fold binding (see "Single-Fold Binding" on page 94).

4. Make and attach a hanging sleeve, if desired.

5. Make, sign, and date a label and attach it to the back of your quilt.

❧ easy marking ❧

I used a Clover fine white marking pen (#517) and a ruler to draw the crosshatched lines on the quilt top before layering and basting. You could machine quilt in this same manner for an old-fashioned look.

❧

JO'S FAVORITE QUILTMAKING TECHNIQUES

For the quilts in this book, you'll need basic rotary-cutting and machine-piecing skills. If you need assistance with either of those, I recommend you go to ShopMartingle.com/HowtoQuilt for free downloadable information. Here I'll cover the specific appliqué and techniques I use in all my quilts.

Prewashing Fabric

Many people ask me if I prewash my fabrics. Yes, I do prewash them all, for several reasons. Whether I'm sewing by hand or machine, I prefer the way prewashed fabric handles during the process of piecing or appliquéing. The fabric weave tightens up during the washing and drying process and not only makes it easier to handle, but also makes it less likely to ravel. Prewashing gets rid of any chemicals used in the finishing process. I generally don't work with precut fabrics; if you do, you may not want to prewash those.

When I wash a fabric, I don't just rinse it out in the sink to see if it bleeds. I wash the fabric with my regular laundry soap, using the gentle wash cycle and cold water. I run it through the entire cycle and then place it in the dryer on the permanent press setting until it's almost dry. Overdrying fabric may set in wrinkles. After I take fabric out of the dryer, I fold it immediately and place it on the shelf. I press the fabric when I'm ready to cut it for a project.

Accurate Sewing and Piecing

Accuracy is important to ensure that the blocks in these smaller-scale quilts will go together nicely. It starts with accurate cutting and continues with accurate piecing. There are several factors to consider when machine piecing to maintain accuracy.

Start by using a *scant* ¼" seam allowance. Why scant? When you press your seam allowances, the fold of the fabric takes up part of the seam and

creates a small amount of "shrinkage." The more seams you have, the more shrinkage occurs. By sewing one or two threads less than an exact ¼", you can compensate for the fold. So, let *scant* be your friend!

Thread can also create added bulk in your seam allowance that can cause inaccuracy. A finer weight will create less bulk for flatter, more accurate seams. I prefer a 60-weight, 100% cotton thread like Presencia or Aurifil. These are both high-quality threads for hand or machine piecing. They are both made from long-staple Egyptian cotton, which makes them stronger than threads that use short-staple fibers, and they also create less lint.

I machine piece my blocks with one of my Pfaff sewing machines. All of these machines have a dual-feed mechanism and I engage it to keep my seams straight and keep the fabric layers from shifting. This mechanism is also helpful when sewing over seam intersections, especially diagonal seams, which can be difficult. Before I owned a Pfaff machine, I used a walking foot to keep seams straight and on track.

∾ clipping trick ∾

At the intersection of the seams, clip into the seam allowance almost to the stitching on each side, ¼" from the seam (the clips will be ½" apart). The clips should be lined up with the outside edge of the seam allowance. Press the seam allowances open between the clips.

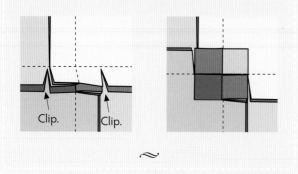

Back-Basting Appliqué

Renowned quiltmaker Jeana Kimball calls this method *template-free*, because there's no need for any type of template-making material. You'll create the appliqués directly from the design that you trace onto the background fabric. A couple of the benefits of this technique are that your pieces will be correctly positioned and your appliqués will lie flatter. Be sure to read through the instructions first to gain an understanding of the technique before beginning.

WHAT YOU'LL NEED

Supplies are minimal, but here's what I recommend.

- **Vellum or another type of see-through paper.** This is used to trace the master pattern.

- **Fine-line permanent marker.** I like Pigma Micron sizes 03 and 05.

- **Mechanical pencil with 0.7 mm or 0.9 mm lead.** A finer lead, such as 0.5 mm, will drop into the weave and is more apt to stretch the fabric.

- **Clover white marking pen.** This is a water-soluble, fine-tip marker, item #517. It's the only removable marking tool that I trust. I know that the marks will disappear.

- **Waxed quilting thread.** Use a color that contrasts with appliqué fabrics for basting.

- **Scissors.** Use a good pair of small, sharp scissors for cutting fabric and clipping threads. My favorite are Dovo 5" sewing scissors.

- **50- or 60-weight thread.** Choose colors that match the appliqués.

- **Jeana Kimball's sizes 9 and 11 straw needles.** These needles are made especially for appliqué and are available at quilt shops and online (JeanaKimballQuilter.com).

- **Needle threader.** This is optional, but I highly recommend the Clover Desk Needle Threader to save your eyes.

PREPARING AND BASTING

Don't be misled by the word *basting*. Basting means to temporarily secure two fabrics together. While this is often done with a long running stitch, it does not define the term, and in this case it's necessary to use a shorter stitch length. The combination of the large needle and the heavy quilting thread perforates the fabric to create a memory line for turning under the fabric when you appliqué.

1. Cut out the background piece 2" larger than the desired finished size. For a block that finishes at 4" square, cut a 6" square.

2. Use a fine-line permanent marker to trace the appliqué pattern onto vellum or another type of see-through paper.

❧ hints for great appliqué ❧

The preceding appliqué instructions show you how I do back-basting appliqué with one particular shape. There are times when you may be working with layered pieces or narrow points. Here are some additional tips that you may find helpful.

Layered Appliqué

When a portion of one appliqué is underneath another appliqué, do not turn under the seam allowance within the overlapped area. This will prevent a ridge that will show through. You may want to trim the seam allowance to be a bit narrower, but by not turning the edge under, the appliqué on top will remain smooth and flat.

Stitching Points

At inner and outer points, I use the Clover white marking pen and mark over the basting thread on the right side of the fabric. This gives me a line to follow when the basting thread is removed, and I know how far to stitch and clip. The water-soluble white line from this pen will disappear with heat from an iron or when washed. Follow the instructions that come with the pen. You can also eyeball the points. They don't have to be exact, and your appliqué will still look great!

Leaving Background Intact

I don't cut away any of the background fabric behind the appliqués. The antique quilts I have examined include backgrounds that are intact. I feel you lose the stability of the block when the background has been cut away, but this is a personal choice, not a rule.

3. Flip the traced design over to the unmarked side. You will be able to see the reversed design through the paper. Place the paper on a light box or another light source so the reversed side is face up. Center the background fabric, with wrong side up, over the traced image.

4. With the mechanical pencil, trace the design onto the wrong side of the background fabric.

5. Looking at the pattern, determine the appliqué stitching sequence. Plan to stitch the shapes that go under other pieces first.

6. Cut a piece of fabric for the first appliqué; it should be large enough to cover the entire area to be appliquéd with enough extra for a seam allowance. Place the piece on the right side of the background fabric over the traced appliqué shape. Hold the background fabric up to the light so you can make sure the correct area is covered completely. Pin the fabric in place.

7. Thread a size 9 straw needle with an 18" length of waxed thread, but do not knot it. Using a short running stitch (9 to 10 stitches per inch) and working from the wrong side, baste the appliqué fabric to the background, stitching directly on the marked line of the shape. Start along a straight edge if possible and leave a 1½" to 2" thread tail at the beginning and end. Do this whenever you start and end a length of thread.

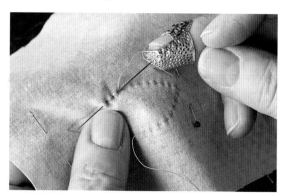

❧ baste today, ❧ appliqué tomorrow

I recommend basting one evening, letting the piece sit overnight, and then proceeding with the appliqué process the following evening. This gives time for the perforation to set. You won't see the perforation when you stitch, but the appliqué will turn under nicely along the perforation created by the basting.

❧

8. Turn the piece to the right side. Using your small, sharp scissors, cut away the excess appliqué fabric, leaving a fat ⅛" seam allowance.

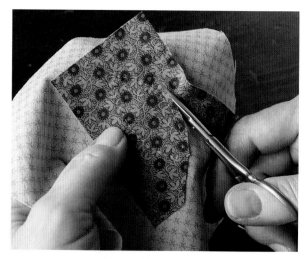

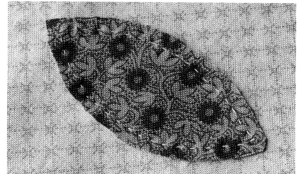

APPLIQUÉING

Stitch the pieces in stages. When appliqués are side by side or layered, you'll need to baste the other pieces first. After appliquéing them in place, go back and baste the remaining pieces.

1. Thread a size 11 straw needle with an 18" length of 50- or 60-weight thread to match or blend with the appliqué fabric. Knot one end of the thread. You'll be working with a single strand.

2. Starting at a basting thread tail and preferably on a straight edge, use your threaded sewing needle to pull the basting thread to the top, and then pull out two or three stitches.

3. Insert the needle into the perforation line from the wrong side of the appliqué fabric. This will hide the knot between the appliqué fabric and the background fabric. Use your needle to turn under the seam allowance. See how the fabric turns under along the basting line? Like magic! Hold the folded edge in place with the thumb of your nonsewing hand.

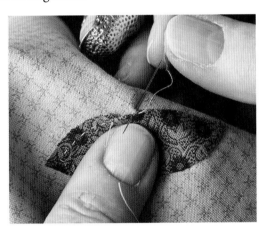

4. Insert the needle into the background fabric as close as possible to where the thread came out of the fold. Bring the needle up through the folded edge of the appliqué, about 1⁄16" away. Just barely catch the folded edge of the appliqué piece so that the thread will not be seen.

5. Take a couple more stitches in the same manner, and then remove a few more basting stitches.

Turn that section under and continue stitching around the entire shape in this manner, referring to "Stitching Points" (page 91) as needed. Remove only one or two basting stitches at a time so your appliqué edges will be smooth.

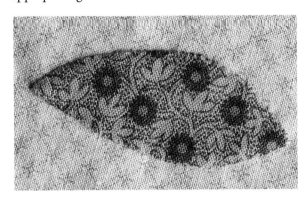

6. To end your stitching, insert the needle into the background next to the appliqué edge and pull the thread to the wrong side. Wrap the thread around the needle twice, hold the needle down next to fabric, and then pull the needle and thread through to create a knot just on top of the fabric. Insert your needle where the thread came out and take it back to the right side, pulling gently to bury the knot between the background fabric and the appliqué fabric. Carefully clip the thread next to the fabric.

7. Continue adding appliqués in this manner, working from the bottom layer to the top.

Cutting Borders

I recommend cutting borders along the lengthwise grain of the fabric, parallel to the selvage. This has the least amount of stretch and will give your quilt nice, straight edges. I seldom recommend cutting borders crossgrain due to the stretch in the fabric. If you do, long may your borders wave.

There are always exceptions to this rule, however, such as when using a stripe cut crosswise for effect. If you do cut crosswise, I would suggest stay stitching to prevent the outer edges from stretching. You know the saying "an ounce of prevention." Keeping a problem from happening is much better than fixing it after it occurs.

Batting

I use 100% cotton batting for my quilts. I recommend cotton batting because it contributes to the flat, antique look and feel that I prefer. Cotton needles wonderfully for hand quilting and lends a vintage appearance to machine quilting.

Single-Fold Binding

I like to use single-fold binding on all my quilts. Double-fold binding is too heavy for most small quilts and can contribute to a wavy edge. I also use a single-fold binding on large quilts. I usually find this type of binding on nineteenth-century quilts and believe if it was good enough for them, it's good enough for me.

To prevent the binding from stretching, I recommend using a walking foot or engaging the dual-feed mechanism, if you have one built into your machine.

1. Cut the number of 1⅛"-wide strips necessary to go around your quilt, adding 10" extra for seaming. Cut the strips crosswise (across the width of the fabric, from selvage to selvage). Using a diagonal seam, join the short ends, right sides together, to make one long piece. Press the seam allowances open.

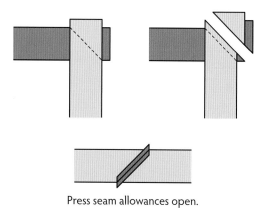

Press seam allowances open.

2. With right sides together, align a raw edge of the binding with the raw edge of the quilt. Beginning about 4" to 5" from the binding end, sew the binding to the quilt using a ¼" seam allowance. Stop sewing ¼" from the corner; backstitch and remove the quilt from the machine.

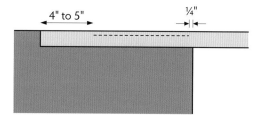

3. Rotate the quilt one quarter turn so you'll be ready to stitch the next side. Fold up the binding at a 90° angle.

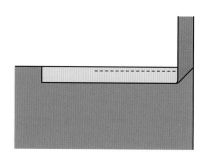

4. Next, fold the binding back down over the first fold and align the binding raw edge with the quilt raw edge. Reposition the quilt under the presser foot. Beginning with a backstitch, continue sewing the binding to the quilt top. Sew until you are ¼" from the next corner; backstitch. Repeat the folding and stitching steps at each corner.

5. Stop sewing about 5" or 6" from the start. Remove the quilt from the machine.

6. Fold the beginning of the binding strip toward the center of the quilt at a 90° angle. Repeat, folding the end of the binding strip toward the edge of the quilt at a 90° angle, leaving about a ⅛" gap between the folds. Press. By leaving the gap, you ensure that the binding will lie nice and flat.

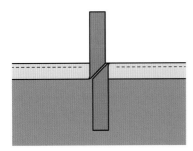

7. Align the fold lines, right sides together, and pin them in place. Sew on the fold line, backstitching at the beginning and end. Trim the excess binding strip, leaving a ¼" seam allowance. Press the seam allowances open. Finish sewing the binding in place.

8. Trim the batting and backing even with the quilt edges. Fold the binding away from the quilt and turn the raw edge under ¼". Fold the binding over the quilt edge and pin it in place so it covers the first stitches, mitering corners as you go when turning.

9. Blindstitch the binding to the quilt back, using small, closely spaced stitches and being careful not to stitch through to the front of the quilt. I recommend taking three or four extra stitches on the folds of the mitered corners to hold them in place.

Use single-fold binding on small quilts to avoid overly bulky edges.

ABOUT THE AUTHOR

Jo Morton is a quiltmaker, fabric designer, teacher, author, and lecturer. Her use of color and design, as well as her fine stitchery, gives her quilts the feeling of having been made in the nineteenth century. Using an antique quilt as a source of inspiration, she creates a new interpretation. Her quilts complement both country and contemporary settings, and her work is included in private and public collections across the country.

In 1980 Jo took her first quilting class, and in 1985 she created her first "made to look old" quilt. She determined early on that if she ever hoped to make all the quilts she wanted to make, they would have to be small, and this size works perfectly in the tiny 1929 bungalow where she lives.

Jo is well known for her "Jo's Little Women Club" patterns, available through participating quilt shops since 2003. Her quilts have appeared in numerous magazines, and she's made several television appearances.

Jo lives in Nebraska City with her husband, Russ, and her kitty, Chloe. Visit JoMortonQuilts.com to learn more, and follow Jo on Instagram at joquilts.